CoNtemporaRy DeCouPAGe

D0317370

6 i.50

Contemporary Decoupage

LINDA BARKER

CHANCELLOR
PRESS

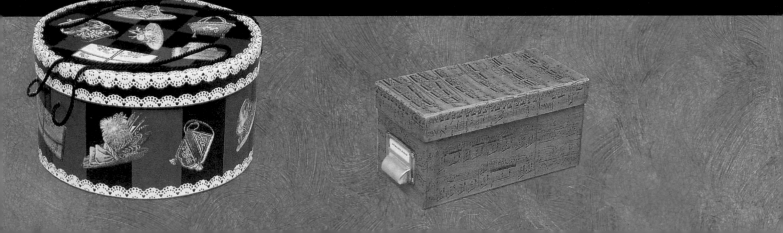

A QUANTUM BOOK

This edition published in 2000 by
Chancellor Press
An imprint of Bounty Books,
a division of
Octopus Publishing Group Ltd
2-4 Heron Quays
London
E14 4JP

Copyright ©MCMXCVI
Quarto Publishing plc

ISBN 0-75370-356-4

QUMCND

This book was produced by
Quantum Publishing
6 Blundell Street
London N7 9BH

Printed and bound in China
by
Leefung-Asco Printers Ltd

Basic Techniques

Friezes, Wallpapers, Screens

Around the House

Furniture

Ornaments, Boxes, & blanks

Contents

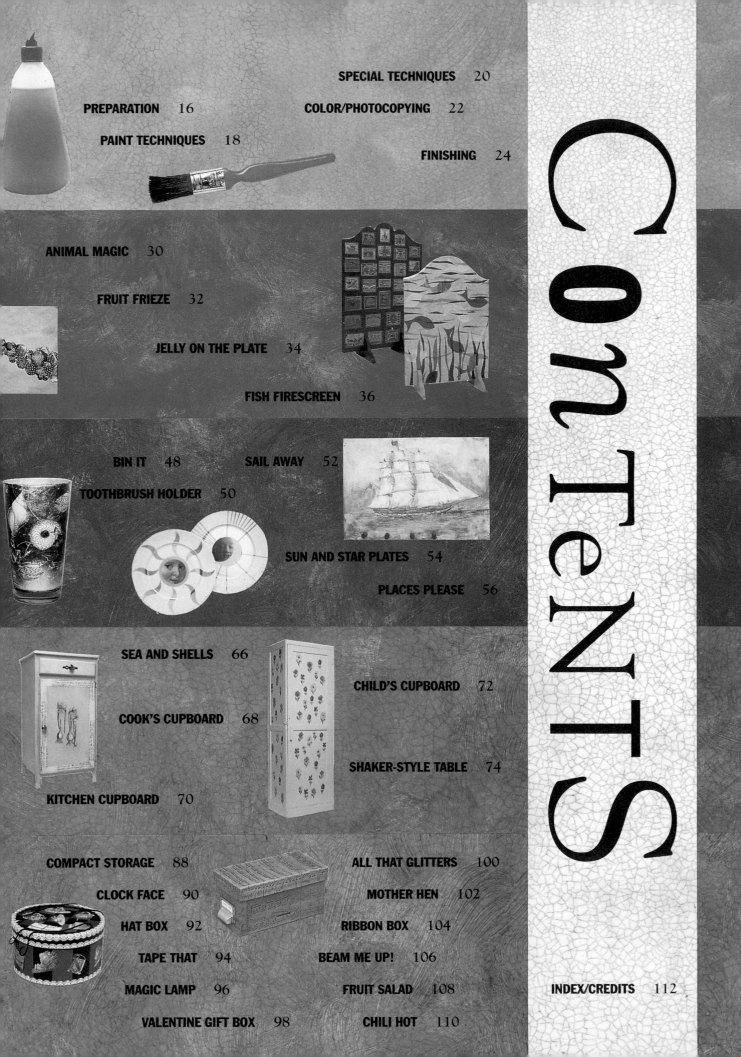

Basic Techniques

Design iDEAS

Color magazines, advertising leaflets, catalogs, and wrapping paper are all excellent sources for decoupage, and so are maps, music scores, and greeting cards. Traditional decoupage made use of seventeenth and eighteenth-century paper designs. These illustrations are still available today in copyright-free source books

Decoupage scraps

These scraps are generally sold as individual sheets and are partially cut out. They often feature Victorian-style images as well as more general flowers and butterflies.

Sheet music

Black-and-white sheet music gives a striking monochrome effect, or you can colorwash it with sepia ink for instant "aging," ideal for classical music.

Flowers

Floral designs are traditional subjects for decoupage. Cut them out from wallpaper, wrapping paper, magazines, and calendars.

Maps and sea charts are perfect for decorating larger items and for creating decoupage with a more masculine, less flowery, look. Available from stationery and specialist stores.

which are ideal for photocopying. Children's coloring books and comics are excellent images to use for nursery furniture. For a unique one-of-a-kind project, make photocopies of your children's drawings. Even newspapers are suitable for decoupage. Use a photocopier to print the chosen text on paper as newsprint tends to be flimsy and porous.

Wrapping paper

There is a huge selection of papers to choose from in a variety of images and styles. Purchase several sheets and keep for future use. Choose good-quality paper; cheaper paper is more porous.

Keeping on the right side of the law

Before copying any design from a book, magazine, greeting card, or wrapping paper, you should check whether or not the design is in copyright. Publishers are generally happy to grant permission for use provided your design is not to be sold or for commercial use.

Greeting cards

Postcards and greeting cards are readily available in an enormous variety of traditional and modern designs. Start your own collection of beautiful cards. You may need to remove the image from the backing card by soaking.

Copyright-free prints

A large number of copyright-free source books covering various styles are available. They are generally printed in black and white, and are ideal for photocopying.

PAPERS

A browse around a stationery or art supply store will reveal another wealth of source material. An art store is an Aladdin's cave, filled with inspirational colors and unusual papers. Once you become hooked on decoupage, you will start to horde all sorts of material that will be useful to you. Foreign paper money,

Drawings or paintings

Children's drawings are particularly suitable for decoupage. Black-and-white drawings can be copied and then colored for use on walls or furniture, or pictures themselves can be cut up for decoupage, although sometimes it is a shame to destroy the original.

Wrapping paper

Bright and cheerful images can be used for children's furniture. Fruit and flowered papers are used for so many things that it is almost impossible to have too many.

Calendars and picture diaries

These are good sources of images, particularly those that reproduce old colored prints. Botanical prints are familiar images used for calendars and are often faithful color reproductions of the original. Be aware of the copyright laws which prevent misuse of protected images. If the work is intended for your own pleasure and not intended for sale, copyright laws have probably not been infringed.

stamps from far-flung places, decorative stationery; all manner of things will suddenly take on a new meaning as you start to look at them with a new perspective. Some food packaging is particularly decorative. Doilies, wrappings, and candy papers are all basic commodities that usually get thrown away, but all are potentially useful. Squirrel everything away in a box and be inspired by it later on.

Photocopies

The photocopier is a decoupager's dream. In addition to enlarging or reducing, copiers can copy multiples of the same image. They also prevent the cutting up of old prints. Color photocopiers are useful, but are inevitably more expensive. However, for an occasional special image, to be used perhaps in the center of your decoupaged item, it could be worth the extra expense.

Postcards and greeting cards

These are also useful sources of interesting images. If the card is too thick – as is usually the case – you will need to peel the thicker back of the card off carefully. Soak the card in a dish of warm water for a few minutes, then peel away the backing paper. Dry the print carefully on absorbent paper.

Inspiration

Almost any printed image can be used for decoupage. Pictures cut from glossy color magazines are perfectly suited. Look for specialist magazines as well as those you may normally purchase; most news stands will stock a good selection. Magazines devoted to birds, gardens, and wildlife are excellent sources for decoupage material.

equipment

Scissors are the most essential piece of equipment to the craft. Some people prefer to use a scalpel or craft knife. Practice your cutting technique using a scalpel and a cutting mat to see which cutting method you prefer. Pinking shears and deckle-edged scissors, which produce a wavy edge, can all be

You need to use craft knives on a cutting mat to protect the surface. They come with replacement blades.

Use colored inks to tint black-and-white photocopies. They come in a choice of colors and give a transparent finish.

You can add gilding powder to the final coat of varnish. Available in several metallic colors.

Finish your decoupage with up to twenty coats of polyurethane varnish for a really hardwearing sheen. Leave to dry between coats.

Household paint-brushes are ideal for covering larger areas with paint and varnish. Clean with the appropriate brush cleaner.

Apply aging varnish to give your items an "aged" look. Brush on and leave to dry. Available from art suppliers.

Vernis à vieillir
Ageing varnish

useful for producing unusual effects. If you are using predominantly black-and-white images, you may need to color some prints. Use watercolors or colored crayons for the best effects, although colored inks and even soft pastels could be used. But avoid wax crayons, which will resist the protective layers of varnish and spoil the project. A selection of fine artists' brushes for coloring and tinting the images is essential.

A tape measure is essential for accuracy when you are placing decoupage in a regular pattern such as a border.

Watercolors and children's paints give a soft colorwash to photocopies. Keep the paint fairly dry to keep the paper from wrinkling.

Use the scissors you find most comfortable – as long as they are sharp. Manicure scissors are perfect for cutting out details.

Chalk pastels come in a choice of colors and give a soft, matte color. Fix pastel with spray fixative to avoid smudging.

You can add designer's gouache to tint the final coat of varnish. Practice on spare board to test the strength.

Make your own black-and-white designs using calligraphy ink and pen. Ideal for photocopying.

Keep a selection of brushes, from large paste brushes to delicate artists' brushes, to make sure you have the right one.

Colored pencils are widely available and easy to use. Shade evenly to avoid lines of color appearing.

Mix your paint colors in special paint dishes or saucers. Always mix enough for the project to avoid variations of shade.

CuttING

Once you have chosen your images, cut them out approximately from the page using large scissors; then cut the smaller details with a smaller pair of scissors, such as manicure scissors, or with a scalpel or craft blade. Before cutting, seal the print with a fixative spray or with diluted white glue.

Using scissors

1 Use an ordinary pair of large, straight-edged scissors to cut the print from the surrounding paper. Be careful not to cut into another image that may be of use to you later on. Do not be tempted to start cutting out fine details with these scissors; otherwise, you will end up with ragged, untidy edges.

2 Take the scissors out of the cut and start cutting from underneath the picture. This allows you to see where you are going, important when you are cutting out a large piece of delicate decoupage. Hold the scissors fairly loosely and turn the paper, not the scissors, with the other hand.

Tearing

Although decoupage means "to cut," it is sometimes good to break the rules and try new effects. Tearing paper into shapes allows you to create more random designs, since the results are different each time.

Cutting with a craft knife

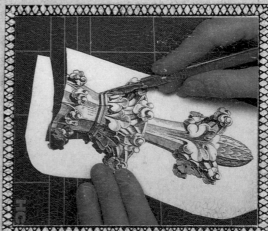

Make sure you cut the image on a self-healing cutting mat, making sure the knife blade is sharp and not damaged. Have a number of spare blades ready; blunt blades will tear the paper. Place the blade against an outline and guide the cutting with your other hand, feeding the paper as you cut.

GLUES

Always choose a water-soluble adhesive, which allows you to remove the cutouts even when they are dry, simply by soaking with water. Polyvinyl acetate (white craft) glue is suitable for most decoupage projects. Wallpaper paste is also suitable. When working with thin or absorbent papers, use only gum arabic.

Using wallpaper paste

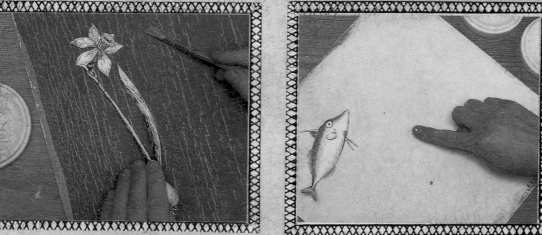

1 Mix a small amount of wallpaper paste according to the instructions on the pack – you will need only the thinnest mix as recommended for lightweight papers. Brush the paste evenly onto the surface to be decorated, covering an area that is slightly larger all around than the cutout.

2 Position the cutout on the pasted area and move it around until the exact position is decided upon. Wipe your hands to remove traces of glue and tamp down the cutout with a damp sponge. Work from the center outward and press down firmly. Rinse the sponge and repeat this procedure.

Using craft glue

1 Pour a little craft glue into a dish. Add cold, clean water to make a consistency of thin cream. Wet your finger and dip it into the thinned glue. Rub it over an area that is slightly larger than the decoupage. Work in more glue, then more water, until the surface is silky smooth. Wipe hands to remove glue.

2 Place the cutout over the glued area, positioning it from the center outward to avoid trapping air bubbles. Carefully move it over the glued surface until it is positioned where you need it. Use a small piece of dampened sponge to tamp down the cutout and remove excess glue.

prePARation

One of the wonderful aspects of decoupage is that almost any surface can be transformed into something quite beautiful. Old painted wooden surfaces should be prepared with a commercial paint and varnish stripper. Once you have stripped off the old paint and varnish, rub the surface with coarse, then medium-grade

Filling holes

1 Old wooden items may have holes or cracks that need to be filled. Using paint stripper first if necessary, rub the surface around the areas to be filled with medium-grade sandpaper. Remove any dust or particles of paint.

2 Using a plaster stripping knife or an old, flexible kitchen knife, apply an all-purpose putty to repair any holes or cracks. Leave the putty to dry, then sand it with fine sandpaper until the surface is perfectly smooth. Use the tips of your fingers to feel for lumps and bumps.

Removing wax or polish

1 You need to remove all wax or polish from the surface; otherwise, the paint will not adhere. Protect the surface on which you are working with sheets of newspaper or heavy-duty plastic sheeting, or work outdoors if possible. Saturate a pad of fine-grade steel wool with mineral spirits.

2 Rub the surface of the wax with the pad. After a few moments, the mineral spirits start to soften the wax. When you notice this happening, start to rub the surface more vigorously until the wax comes off onto the pad. Repeat this procedure until all the wax has been removed.

steel wool. A quick wash with warm soapy water is then all that is needed. Rusty metal containers can also be stripped back and brought back to new life. Wash glass items thoroughly in hot soapy water before adding decoupage. Wash old terracotta using hot soapy water and an abrasive scrubbing pad, and leave overnight in a warm place until absolutely dry.

Removing old paint

1 To remove old paint, protect the surface on which you are working with newspaper or heavy plastic sheeting. Using an old brush, dab the paint stripper onto the painted surface until it is covered with the gel. Work outside if at all possible or in a well-ventilated room to avoid breathing in the fumes.

3 Protect your hands with rubber gloves and use a pad of coarse steel wool to remove the blistered layers of paint. On larger pieces of furniture, you may prefer to use a flat-bladed knife to remove the paint. Dispose of the waste inside layers of newspaper and wrap it well in two plastic bags. Follow any additional disposal instructions that are printed on the label.

2 After a short time, you will see the old layers of paint start to blister and bubble. Don't be impatient – leave the paint stripper on the surface for the full time stated on the can to make sure that it has penetrated right through the paint layers.

PaiNT TechNiques

There are many different paint finishes that enhance decoupage. Generally, you should choose an effect that complements the nature of the decoupage.

Before painting, lightly sand and seal the piece of prepared, stripped furniture with a coat of acrylic primer. Metal objects will need a coat of red

Cutting a sponge

1 You can use a natural sea sponge for sponging; however, they are often expensive, and greater demand for these marine sponges does encourage harvesting live sponges which should be allowed to grow. It is preferable to adapt a regular cellulose sponge. Cut the sponge in half and pull off the smooth sides.

2 Cut into the surface of the sponge with a pair of sharp scissors. The aim is to cut varying sized holes in the surface to imitate the holed, textured surface of a real marine sponge. Pull out smaller pieces of sponge with your fingers to roughen the surface even more.

Colorwashing

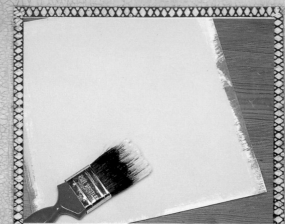

1 This is perhaps the simplest of all paint techniques and creates a soft subtle finish which is perfectly suited to decoupage. Using a paintbrush, apply the base paint color evenly over the prepared and primed surface and allow it to dry.

2 Thin two parts of a paler color with one part of clean, cool water and mix together thoroughly. Decant a little paint into an appropriate container and dip a clean cellulose sponge into it. Wipe the painted surface with the diluted color, applying the color in all directions. Allow to dry.

oxide primer to prevent rust from forming again. When the primer has dried thoroughly, sand lightly with fine-grade sandpaper and apply at least two coats of your chosen base color. If you are happy with this finish, then you can start to apply the decoupage cutouts at this stage. Wherever possible, you should try to use water-based paints, latex (emulsion) paints.

Sponging

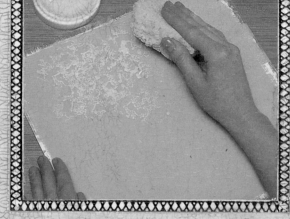

1 First prime the object to be decoupaged with at least one coat of white acrylic primer. Leave to dry thoroughly. If the primer highlights any holes or cracks, repair them using a fine putty, leave to dry, then smooth with fine-grade sandpaper. Apply acrylic primer over the dry putty.

3 Decant a little of the top color into an appropriate container and dip the surface of the sponge into this. Dab the excess paint onto a piece of scrap paper. Lightly pat the surface of the paint with the sponge to transfer the paint. Alter the angle of the sponge each time to keep a pattern from building up.

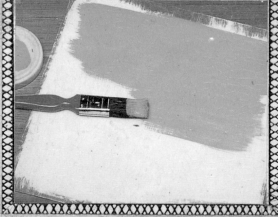

2 Select your base color and brush it over the dried primer. Use a small brush to paint between small joints and corners. Brush the paint evenly to avoid heavy build-up in certain areas. Brush out any drips or runs as they occur, and keep checking the paintwork as it dries to avoid drips.

4 For a softer look, apply a further layer of color using a lighter version of the first sponged color. Use the same technique of applying the paint, altering the angle of the sponge each time to prevent a pattern from building up. Allow to dry thoroughly before starting to apply the decoupage.

SpeciAL teCHNiQUES

Paint techniques need not just be done to add color. They can also be used to "age" your piece of furniture. Distressing creates a well-worn finish by partially removing the top layer of paint to reveal the paint or wood underneath. It is usual to create this effect along the edges of furniture and around

Distressing

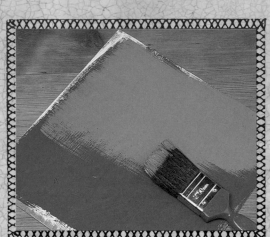

1 Prime the object with a layer of white acrylic primer. Brush on your chosen base color paint, making sure that the white primer coat does not show through. In some cases, you may need to apply a second coat to give adequate coverage. Leave to dry.

3 Paint on the second layer of color. The wax layer underneath will have the effect of resisting the top layer of paint, so do not worry that this layer will dry unevenly. Apply only one layer of color – it will seem slightly patchy.

2 Rub the dried paint surface with a regular household candle to provide a resistant layer. Do not follow a regular pattern, but aim to cover the surface with childlike scribbles, using a strong horizontal or vertical movement.

4 When the top layer is dry, there may be a few areas that will not dry completely as explained. Start to rub the surface all over with fine-grade sandpaper. The paint applied over the wax scribbles will remove easily, resulting in a distressed finish.

handles, where in time the paint would naturally wear away. Here we show how to create a distressed look by using candle wax to stop the top layer of paint from adhering to the surface. The paint is then simply rubbed away.

Another "old" technique is a crackle finish. This is done by applying a coat of crackle varnish between the top two layers of paint. When the top coat of paint dries, it will form strong cracks to reveal the paint color underneath.

Crackle finish

1 Prepare the surface of your piece of furniture or object for painting as before and paint with a layer of white acrylic primer. Brush on at least one coat of your chosen base paint color, preferably two coats to give a good even coverage.

3 Apply the top paint color. Use a wide brush if possible and apply the color evenly, following a left-to-right pattern. Do not go back over previous brush marks; this will disturb the varnish underneath. As the top coat dries, strong cracks will appear to give a wonderful aged appearance.

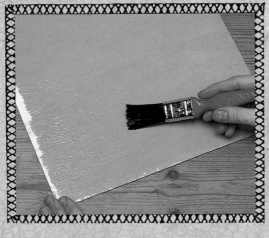

2 Brush on a thin layer of transparent crackle varnish. Work methodically – you need to make sure there is a good coverage of varnish, but not too heavy. Brush the varnish out in all directions and allow to dry.

Color

Instead of leaving black-and-white images plain, it is possible to apply color to the prints before gluing them in place. Almost any medium can be used to color the prints, with the exception of oil-based colors which will resist the subsequent layers of varnish.

Soft pastels

Soft pastels come in a choice of colors and give a lovely soft finish to the images. The colors can be blended gently with your fingertip to create a muted effect. Do not use wax crayons; they will resist the protective varnish.

Watercolor paints

Watercolor paints are perfect for coloring black-and-white prints, giving a subtle color. Use a fine artist's brush and leave the prints to dry thoroughly before sealing and cutting out.

Colored inks

Colored inks, too, can be useful, particularly when you need transparent yet strong color. Apply the ink carefully with a fine artist's brush. Leave to dry before spraying with fixative to seal.

Colored pencils

Colored pencils are widely available in a good choice of colors and are very easy to use. Shade evenly to avoid lines of color. It doesn't matter if you color over the outer edges as the image is cut out after shading.

Photocopying

Without a doubt the photo-copier has made decoupage infinitely easier and considerably cheaper. With the wealth of copyright-free black-and-white source books available today, the photocopier is invaluable.

Sealing images

To keep the printing inks from "bleeding" when you glue the cutouts, seal them first with a liquid or aerosol fixative. Pastel, charcoal, or watercolor fixatives are available from artists' supply stores.

Changing sizes

You can enlarge or reduce pictures to suit your project. Enlargements of enlargements are also possible, although the image will start to deteriorate after a certain number of enlargements (depending on the condition of the original image).

Stretching

Some photocopiers also enable you to "stretch" an image to give you a picture of the correct shape. This can give a longer, thinner picture. If possible, ask your local copy shop to demonstrate the facilities of their machine.

Normal size

A bit longer . . .

Changing color

Color photocopiers make their copies in four color stages – cyan (blue), magenta (red), yellow, and black – to produce every color. They can also be used to print in one color only.

Full color copy

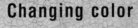

Negative colors

FINishing

This is the final treatment that will really bring your piece of decoupage to life. If the step-by-step instructions suggest applying fifteen layers of varnish, this may seem excessive, but with spray varnishes and easy-to-use acrylic varnishes, the whole process isn't as tortuous as it may seem.

Cracklelure varnish

1 Apply the first coat of the cracklelure varnish. Apply the second part of the varnish, which is a water-based crackling varnish. Allow it to dry. After a short while, you will notice fine cracks appearing on the surface.

2 When the varnish is completely dry, rub a little burnt umber oil paint over the surface of the cracks to highlight them. Remove excess oil paint as you progress so that the oil paint is retained only in the tiny cracks.

Removing excess adhesive

Before varnishing, when the paper motif has been glued onto its surface, take care to remove any excess adhesive from around the edge. Use a small damp sponge and practice a gentle rocking movement. Rinse the sponge in cool clean water if you get a build up of adhesive.

Acrylic varnish

Once the decoupage is completely dry, start to apply the layers of varnish. Decant a little acrylic varnish into a saucer and brush it over the cutout. Leave to dry. Repeat until seven coats have been applied.

Polyurethane varnish tends to color the paper slightly and will often yellow slightly with age, but this quality can add an appealing antiqued look. Water-based acrylic varnish is simple to use but has a harder finish that is stable and will not mellow. It is possible to tint varnish with oil paint. Blend a little color with mineral spirits, then add it to the polyurethane varnish. Use thinned gouache and water to tint acrylic varnishes.

Antiquing with wax

To achieve an antiqued look, use a dark wax to deepen the finish. Apply layers of protective varnish in the usual way, when the top layer is completely dry rub the surface with a pad of medium-gauge wire wool to roughen the surface.

Spray polyurethane varnish

The main advantage for using this type of varnish is that it is wonderfully quick and easy to use. As with regular brush on polyurethane varnish, you need to allow each coat to dry before applying the next, but the layering up process is much quicker and less tiresome, with the advantage being no brushes to clean.

Polyurethane varnish

When the cutouts are totally dry, apply successive layers of polyurethane varnish, allowing each layer to dry completely before applying the next. Build up at least seven coats of varnish, but aim for a maximum of twenty.

Vernis à vieillir
Ageing varnish

Friezes, Wallpapers, Screens

foliage FRIEZE

This frieze emulates the grand hand-painted floral swags that are seen in some of the grand houses of Europe. It is perfectly suited for a bedroom or a living room.

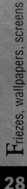
You will need

Wallpaper/wrapping paper or any source material with foliage

Small, sharp scissors

String and chalk

All-purpose glue

Acrylic varnish

Small sponge

Watercolors

1 Select your source material, and cut around the foliage details using a pair of small sharp scissors. You will need smaller pieces of foliage for the ends of each swag, but you can use larger groups for the center areas.

2 Measure the length of one wall that you are covering with the decoupage. Determine the number of swags you would like to feature, and divide the wall measurement by the number of swags to determine the width of each swag. Mark these points with chalk along the wall.

3 Tape a length of string between two points, allowing it to swag in the middle. Use chalk to draw this curve on the wall, then remove the string and repeat between the other points, making sure the drop of each swag is the same.

4 Apply the glue to the wall and rub with your finger until silky smooth. Press the pieces of foliage onto the glued surface and wipe off the excess glue with a small piece of sponge squeezed out in warm water. Continue the process until each swag is finished. Allow to dry; then lightly tint with watercolors.

Other ideas

For a softer look you could use flowers as well as foliage within the swags.

Chalk is used to figure out the measurements for these elegant grapes and vine leaves.

αniMAL MAGiC

This is a perfect alternative for the expensive wallpapers available for nurseries and children's rooms. If you have any older children, use their hand-drawn animal pictures for the paper; otherwise, select images from story books or comics.

You will need

Children's pencil drawings or comic/story book sources

Plain white paper

Colored crayons/ watercolors

Sealer (fixative)

Scissors

Carpenter's level and chalk

All-purpose glue

Small sponge

Acrylic varnish

1 Select the images to go on the wall. Measure the wall area to be covered and calculate the number of images you will need. If you are using drawn images like the ones shown here, photocopy each animal at the black-and-white stage onto white paper and then color each animal using crayons or watercolors.

2 If using watercolor, when the colors are dry, seal the prints using fixative. This prevents the colors from bleeding when the acrylic varnish is applied. Cut out the animals using a pair of sharp scissors, following the outlines carefully. Turn the paper, not the scissors, when cutting out to ensure a smooth cut edge.

3 Draw a line with ordinary white chalk on the wall which will be the base line for all the animals' feet. Use a level for accuracy. Apply a little glue to a section of the wall, rubbing it until it is silky and smooth. Dip your finger in water and rub it into the glue to make it perfectly silky smooth. Apply each animal cutout over it and smooth from the center outward to avoid trapping any air bubbles.

4 Build up the motifs and remove excess glue from the wall as you progress using a small piece of sponge squeezed out in warm water. Once the glue has dried, apply at least two coats of acrylic varnish, allowing the first coat to dry thoroughly before applying subsequent coats.

Other ideas

Use the same animal images to decorate the sides of a toy chest or across the drawers of a piece of furniture.

Prints, like these birds, are also good source material for decoupage.

fRUIT frieze

Look out for beautiful fruit prints in antique and junk markets and use photocopies of these for your source material. The frieze can be pasted on the wall at a normal chair rail height or at a higher level just below the ceiling.

You will need

Black-and-white fruit prints

Plain white paper

Scissors

Sealer (fixative)

Colored crayons/ watercolors

All-purpose glue

Small sponge

Acrylic varnish

1 Select your source material and photocopy enough of the images to cover the area you have chosen to decoupage. Color the copies using either crayons or watercolors. To avoid wrinkles on the paper, do not use too much water when using watercolors. Leave to dry.

2 Seal the color on the copies using charcoal, pastel or watercolor fixative which can be purchased from an art supplier. When dry, cut out each fruit piece using a pair of sharp narrow-bladed scissors. Turn the paper, not the scissors, to ensure a smooth cutting line.

3 Apply the glue directly to the wall in small workable sections. Rub the glue with your finger until it feels silky smooth. Dip the end of your finger in water and work it into the glue until perfectly smooth. Place the cutouts over the glue.

4 Press each cutout with your fingers from the center outward to avoid trapping air bubbles. Overlap the pieces where necessary, applying more glue in the same way if it is needed. Gradually build up the frieze until you are satisfied with the overall effect.

5 Wipe off excess glue as you continue along the frieze, using a small piece of sponge squeezed out in warm water. Protect the finished frieze using two or three coats of acrylic varnish. Allow the first coat to dry thoroughly before applying the second.

Other ideas

A vegetable frieze would work just as well if fruit source material is difficult to find.

A jolly vegetable frieze brightens up any kitchen. Wipe off excess glue along the frieze with a sponge.

jelly on the plate

You can easily create wonderful wallpaper effects with minimum expense using ordinary photocopies. You will need a lot of black-and-white copies, so it is quicker and more cost-effective to group many images together on one sheet.

You will need

Plumb line

Cardboard

Jelly motifs, such as from a source book of copyright images

Small, sharp scissors

All-purpose glue

Colored crayons/ watercolors

Sealer (fixative)

Small sponge

Acrylic varnish

1 Mark the wall with a regular grid before photocopying the motifs. Hang a plumb line from the ceiling and place a square of cardboard behind the string. Holding the cardboard diagonally, align two corners of the square with the vertical. Mark the four points of the square. Repeat until a regular grid is marked around the room.

2 Select the motifs to be used for the wallpaper effect. Each point marked on the wall represents a motif, so you will need to photocopy as many jelly mold motifs as there are points on the wall. Use colored crayons or watercolors to tint the copies lightly, but do not allow the copies to become too wet.

3 When dry, seal the copies to keep the color from bleeding when the varnish is applied. Most art suppliers sell charcoal, pastel, or watercolor fixative which will act as a sealer. Once it is dry, cut out the motifs using a sharp pair of narrow-bladed scissors.

4 Rub a little glue over the point marked on the wall until the glue is silky smooth. Apply the cutout over this and press from the center outward to avoid trapping any air bubbles. Slide the cutout until it is placed exactly in the center of the mark. Any deviation from this will spoil the regular effect.

5 Blot excessive glue from around each motif using a small sponge squeezed out in warm water. Repeat this procedure until all the wall has been covered with the cutouts. Allow the glue to dry completely; then apply two coats of protective acrylic varnish over the wall to finish.

Use crayons or watercolors to color your photocopied images, like these pretty teacups.

Other ideas

Apply the jelly mold motifs on half the wall only, either above or below a normal chair rail height.

fish fIRE screen

This blank fire screen has been specially bought for decorating. Or, you could use a tired old screen. Here decoupage is used to great effect with tissue paper, providing a semi-transparent material to capture the feeling of the ocean depths.

You will need

Fire screen

Tissue paper in pink, yellow, purple, dark blue, dark green

Tissue paper in sea blue (enough to cover the screen 1½ times)

Craft knife

White latex (emulsion) paint

Sea blue acrylic paint

Paintbrush

Craft glue and brush

Clear satin varnish and brush

1 Paint your blank fire screen with one coat of white latex (emulsion) paint and leave to dry thoroughly. If you are rejuvenating an old screen, make sure that you have sanded and primed the surface.

2 Fold the pink tissue paper into six thicknesses and draw or trace the fish shape on to it using a thick, sharp pencil. Repeat with the yellow tissue. The curvy fish here imply movement in the water, but any shaped fish would do. Cut the purple and dark blue paper into small strips. These will form the flora of the ocean.

3 Carefully cut around the penciled shapes with a craft knife, ensuring that it cuts all the way through the paper. This should give you six fish exactly the same shape in both pink and yellow.

4 Tear the blue tissue paper into four strips, leaving the edges ragged. Coat each strip in glue and paste to the screen, overlapping each strip. This will dry as areas of darker blue, giving a feeling of depth to your ocean. Leave to dry.

Other ideas

A similar marine design would be ideal for the bathroom, decorating a plain cupboard or bath board.

Matchbooks or firework packaging would also be appropriate imagery for a firescreen.

around the
house

LigHT and LacY

This basic lampshade is one of the easiest projects in the book and one that has a really professional look.

You will need

White paper or "plastic" 8in (20cm) tall lampshade

Water-based blue paint

1yd (1m) each of 1½in (4cm) and 2¾in (7cm)-wide cream paper lace

Wallpaper paste and brush

Scissors

Water-based quick-drying matte varnish

1 Apply two coats of blue paint to the lampshade, allowing each coat to dry thoroughly. Measure around the lampshade and divide the top and bottom edges of the shade into eight equal sections. Make a small pencil mark at the top and bottom edges. Measure the paper lace against the height of the lampshade, cutting four pieces of lace in each width which are just long enough to fold over each edge to make a neat finish.

2 Mix a small amount of wallpaper paste, and spread sparingly on the back of one piece of the narrow paper lace and on the lampshade. Position the lace on the lampshade, making sure it is straight. Smooth it gently with your fingers, removing any excess glue or air bubbles, and make sure the edges are stuck down.

3 Following the pencil marks, paste the second piece of narrow lace exactly opposite the first piece and the remaining two in between, thereby quartering the lampshade. Now paste the wider paper lace between the narrower strips. Smooth the strips down carefully and pay particular attention to turning under the edges and sticking them to the inside of the lampshade. This produces a very neat finish. Allow the paste to dry thoroughly.

4 When the shade is completely dry, apply two or three coats of water-based matte varnish, allowing each coat to dry completely before applying the next.

Other ideas

If paper lace is difficult to find, you can use doilies, although you may have to vary the shapes of the lace pieces. The color of paint you choose will determine the look of the shade, making it pastel pretty or rich-looking.

Water-based paints have many cheerful colors to choose from. You can use paper doilies instead of lace for the same attractive look.

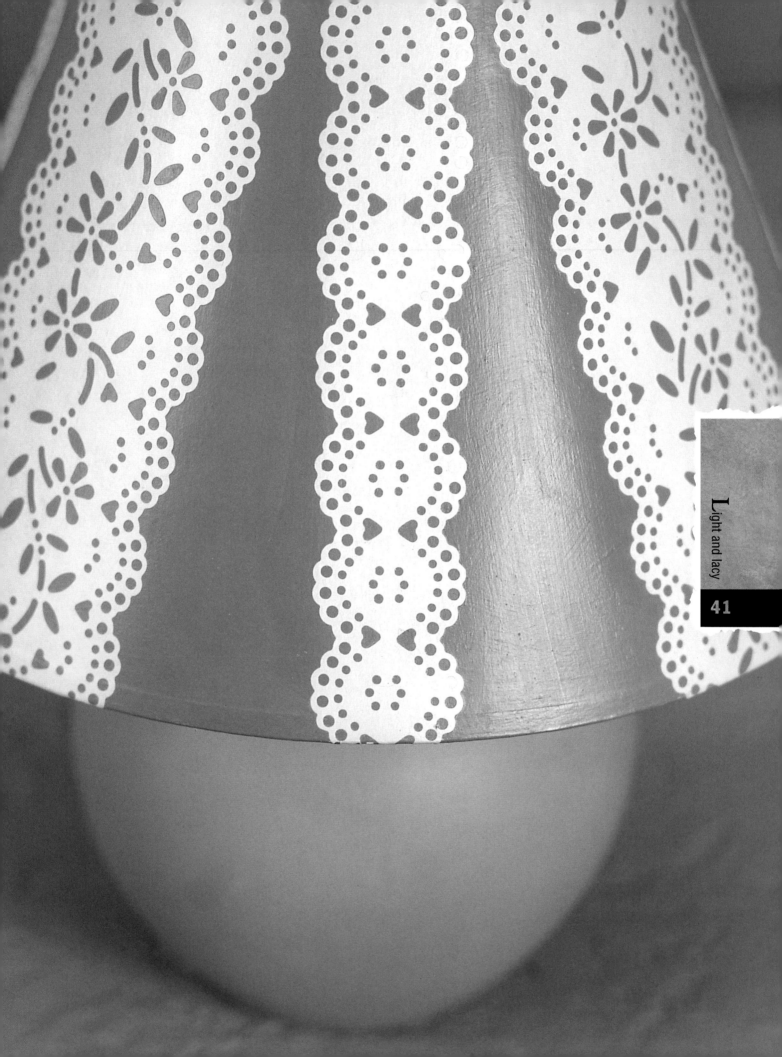

TEA Time

Decorate an elegant and generous tray with images of old cups and saucers cut from wrapping paper. It is a very simple project, but the crackle finish gives it a professional look.

You will need

Unpainted wooden tray

Water-based paint in red and blue

Paintbrush

Wrapping paper

Small scissors

Wallpaper paste

Crackle varnish

Oil paint in burnt umber

Fine sandpaper

Matte polyurethane varnish and brush

Cotton rags

1 Lightly sand the surface of the tray. Dust with a clean, soft brush. Paint the tray with two coats of blue and allow to dry between each coat. Paint the top edge and the inside of the handles with red. Allow to dry.

2 Carefully cut out the shapes from the wrapping paper. If the shapes are complicated, move the paper around, not the scissors, to give a smooth cut edge. Mix up a small amount of wallpaper paste. Arrange the shapes on the base of the tray and then stick in place with the paste. Smooth out any air bubbles and lumps of paste with your fingers. Wipe with a clean cloth and allow to dry.

3 Following the manufacturer's instructions, paint on the first coat of crackle glaze. Allow it to dry, then apply a second coat. As the second coat dries, fine cracks will begin to appear. When the crackle glaze is thoroughly dry, rub a small amount of burnt umber oil paint into the cracks with a rag. Gently rub off the excess oil paint with a second rag and the flat of your hand – it is important to leave a residue in the cracks. Leave at least a day for the oil paint to dry.

4 When the tray is completely dry, apply four coats of matte polyurethane varnish, allowing each coat to dry before applying the next. Lightly sand and dust the third coat of varnish to make the last coat as smooth as possible.

Other ideas

This tray is decorated with cups and saucers to suit a teatime theme, but there is a wonderful selection of wrapping paper available, and you're sure to find lots of inspiration.

Cut out the shapes on the paper very carefully for a really professional effect.

Butt**ER**fly **wings**

Enliven an ordinary glass vase by turning it into a mysterious object full of beautiful creatures. Fill with flowers or simply display as an ornament.

You will need

Semitransparent glass vase

Butterfly pictures

Craft glue

Metallic bronze paint (for painting on glass)

1in (2.5cm) paintbrush

Protective glaze

Steel wool

1 Make several color photocopies of the butterfly pictures. Carefully cut out the butterflies using small, sharp scissors. When cutting out delicate shapes, it is easier to turn the paper, not the scissors, if you are cutting to achieve a smooth edge.

2 Make your selection of cutouts, brush the right side of the butterflies with glue, and stick them to the inside of the vase. Allow the glue to dry thoroughly.

3 Now paint the inside of the vase with two coats of bronze metallic paint, allowing the first coat to dry thoroughly before applying the next. Leave to dry. Apply two coats of protective glaze to the inside of the vase. This will protect the paint from the flower water.

4 Carefully rub the rim of the vase with steel to remove excess paint or glaze.

Note: Because this vase is decorated and painted on the inside, you will need to choose a vase with a wide neck so that you can fit your hand inside comfortably.

Other ideas

Other natural designs such as fish, animals, and flowers would also look good. Choosing other metallic paints would give a different look.

Botanical illustrations would also work well on the vase.

iN the fraME

Stenciling furniture and all manner of household objects was a favorite Victorian pastime. Here a spray technique using real ferns has been used on gold paper to decorate a modern picture frame. It would make an ideal border for a gardening print.

You will need

Fern leaves

Softwood picture frame

Sheet of gold poster paper

Spray paint in brown, light green, and dark green

Scissors

Metal ruler

Craft knife

Spray adhesive

Wallpaper paste

Water-based satin varnish

Fine sandpaper

1 To press the fern leaves, collect some good examples on a dry day and lay them between sheets of absorbent paper between the pages of a heavy book. They should be ready to use in three or four days.

2 Lay the picture frame right side down, on the back of the gold paper. Draw around the frame and the center opening with a pencil.

3 Remove the frame and add enough to the center opening and the outside measurements so that the paper will wrap around the edges of the frame. Cut around this new line using a craft knife and a metal ruler. The frame shown has a molding surrounding the center.

4 Turn the gold paper right side up and spatter the two shades of green paint over the gold surface. Make sure some of the gold still shows through the spattered paint. (You can achieve this by not pressing the nozzle right down on the spray paint can; the paint will then spatter out less evenly.)

5 Arrange the fern leaves over the gold spattered paper. Apply spray adhesive to the back of each leaf and press it in place. When all the leaves are stuck down, spray the whole surface with brown paint. Spray evenly at first, then spatter. Allow a little of the background to show. When dry, lift off the leaves.

6 Apply wallpaper paste to the front surface of the frame and the back of the stenciled paper. Press the paper onto the frame, wrapping the excess to the back. Snip the inside corner so the paper fits neatly inside the center molding on the frame. Smooth the paper down. Allow to dry.

7 The strips of paper for the outside edge of the frame should be wide enough to overlap the back of the frame by ⅖in (1cm). Cover the molding in the center of the frame with similar paper, overlapping into the rabbet (rebate). Allow to dry.

8 Coat the frame with three or four coats of satin varnish, allowing each coat to dry before applying the next. Lightly sand and dust the next-to-last coat to give a smooth finish.

You can also use attractive marbled paper as a background for the fern leaves.

Other ideas

Choose other metallic papers such as silver, copper, or bronze to change the look of the frame.

Bin iT

For a lasting memento of a foreign vacation or business trip, paste receipts and low-denomination paper money onto a plain wastepaper bin – a witty and unusual receptacle in which to jettison those unwanted bills!

You will need

- **A selection of notes and receipts**
- **Metal wastepaper bin**
- **Wallpaper paste**
- **Craft knife**
- **Matte polyurethane varnish and brush**
- **Oil paint in raw umber (optional)**

1 Select a variety of old travel receipts and mix the wallpaper paste according to instructions. Apply a thin layer of paste to the surface of the wastepaper bin and the back of the receipts. Starting at the edge of the bin (top and bottom), lay them onto the bin at slanting angles and smooth out air bubbles or ripples in the paper with your fingers. Work toward the middle of the bin until the whole surface is covered. Use the largest receipts first, leaving the smaller ones to fill in any gaps. Make sure that all the edges are well stuck down.

2 With a sharp craft knife, carefully trim away any pieces overlapping the edge and tuck them under the rolled rim of the bin. If the bin does not have rolled edges, trim the paper level with the top and bottom edges.

3 Paste paper money over the background of receipts. Space them well apart and at different angles. Allow to dry.

4 Apply two or three coats of matte polyurethane varnish to the finished collage, allowing each coat to dry before applying the next. Before applying the final coat of varnish, lightly sand the bin with fine sandpaper to create a smooth finish. Dust with dry brush and then apply the final coat of varnish. To give the bin an interesting aged effect, add a small amount of raw umber oil paint to the final coat of varnish.

Other ideas

As an alternative, use Chinese or Japanese printed papers for an exotic, oriental effect.

Collect interesting packaging and labels from foreign trips, or newspapers with unusual type, and paste these onto the wastepaper bin as a variation.

$t$oothBrush HOLDER

This toothbrush holder started life as an ordinary glass vase, but its shape perfectly suits its new role. Look for a vase with a heavy base which will be stable on a bathroom shelf.

You will need

Glass vase

Denatured alcohol (methylated spirits)

Cotton cloth

Small, sharp scissors

Pictures of shells

Plain white paper

Sealer (fixative)

All-purpose glue

Silver Dutch metal leaf

Spray varnish

1 Clean the glass inside and out using a clean cotton cloth and denatured alcohol (methylated spirits) to remove any traces of grease. From this stage on, try to avoid touching the glass inside the vase as any grease marks will eventually tarnish the silver leaf.

2 Photocopy the shell pictures on white paper and cut out the shells. Apply the glue to the front of the cutout, not to the vase. Place each cutout carefully inside the vase with the image facing outward, to be seen through the glass.

3 Seal the back of the shell cutouts with fixative. When dry, spray the varnish to coat the inside of the vase as evenly as possible. Allow it to dry in a warm place until it remains only slightly tacky but not sticky – rather like tape.

4 Press the silver transfer leaves over the tacky surface. It is unavoidable that the leaves will wrinkle and crease but this is not detrimental to the final effect. Continue until the whole surface is covered then remove the excess leaf with your finger.

5 Spray at least five coats of varnish inside the vase, allowing each coat to dry thoroughly before applying the next. Leave for at least four days before using.

Other ideas

You could use oil-based paint instead of the silver metal leaf, but coat the back of the cutouts with at least four layers of varnish before applying the paint to stop the oil from penetrating the surface of the paper.

Old shell or fossil imagery looks good in most contexts – such as on this notebook.

Sail Away

The handpainted effect on this hook is in fact created from an ordinary photocopy that has been repeatedly worn away with sandpaper and hand tinted until the look has been achieved.

You will need

Small piece of wood or pegboard

Sailing ship picture

Plain white paper

All-purpose glue

Adhesive brush

Water-based paints

Brush

Sandpaper

Sealer (fixative)

Acrylic varnish

Drill with wide bit

Dowel pegs

Wood glue

Rope

1 Photocopy the sailing ship picture on white paper. Cut the wood to size if necessary: the photocopy and the wood should be approximately the same size. Spread glue onto the surface of the wood and paste on the whole photocopy sheet. Smooth the copy with your fingers, from the center outward to avoid trapping air bubbles.

2 When dry, tint the photocopy with thin washes of color. Allow the color to dry, then use fine sandpaper to "distress" the surface of the copy. You will notice that the sandpaper rubs away some of the color also, so reapply and continue this process until you reach the effect you're happy with.

3 Allow the paints to dry thoroughly, then seal with a layer of charcoal, pastel, or watercolor fixative (available from art suppliers). Once this layer is dry, apply at least five coats of acrylic varnish, allowing each coat to dry thoroughly before applying the next.

4 Drill holes at the base of the decoupage picture to about half the depth of the wood. The diameter of these holes should be equal to the diameter of the dowel pegs. Squeeze a little wood glue into each hole before twisting in the dowel peg.

5 Using the same drill bit, drill right through the wood at top right and top left of the picture, if required, to hold rope ties. Insert a length of rope through the holes and knot it neatly at the front of the picture.

Other ideas

Glue the sailboat photocopy to a piece of driftwood for an original look.

Torn paper can be used to suggest the sea and sky. Experiment with different techniques.

Sun AND STAR *plates*

Plates have been decorated from the earliest times and look good displayed on the wall. Brighten up your kitchen or dining room with plain white plates decorated with bold paper designs.

You will need

Plain plate

Gold and silver paper

Small, sharp scissors

Craft glue

Tracing paper

Brush

1 Do not choose a plate with a deep ridge if you intend decorating it all over as it will be difficult to glue on the shapes. Wash the plate thoroughly in hot soapy water to make sure it is grease-free. Rinse and leave to dry.

2 On the back of the gold and silver paper, draw sun and moon shapes. If you do not have the confidence to draw shapes freehand, trace them from a magazine or book. Children's coloring books and embroidery books are good sources of clear, bold shapes suitable for tracing.

3 Cut out the shapes carefully using small, sharp scissors. It is easier to turn the paper, not the scissors, when cutting out small shapes. The faces for the sun and moon shown here were cut from art magazines, but also look in other color magazines for suitable images. Cut out all the pieces and arrange them on the plate. When you have a pleasing design, make guidemarks with a pencil that will wash off easily afterward. Apply glue to the paper pieces. Place the paper shape on the plate, rub it flat with a clean cloth right up to the edges, and wipe off any excess glue using a damp cloth.

4 When dry, apply one or two coats of clear polyurethane varnish to protect the surface. If you use a white plate, be sure to work with clean brushes and clear varnish to avoid a messy finish. These plates are not suitable for food use, but are simply decorations.

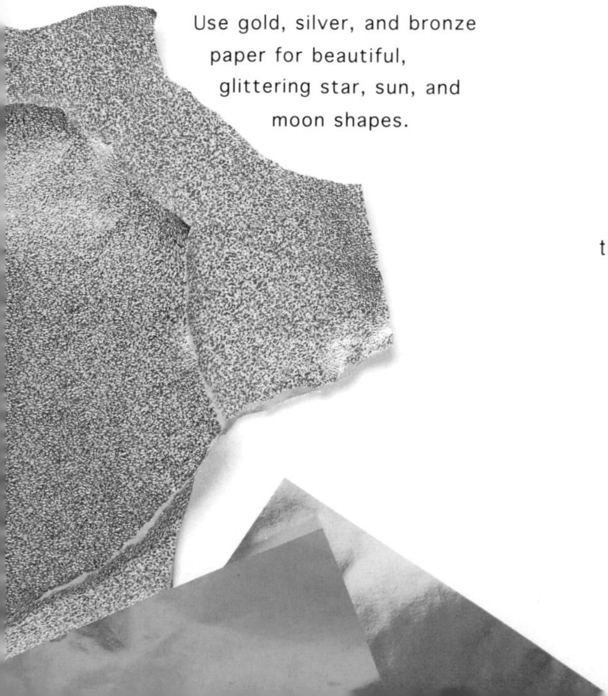

Use gold, silver, and bronze paper for beautiful, glittering star, sun, and moon shapes.

Other ideas

Cut out your own selection of shapes, or use magazine pictures on their own. If you are tracing shapes from books, spray the back of the tracing with spray adhesive and position it on your gold or silver paper, then cut out the shape accurately with small, sharp scissors or use a scalpel and a cutting mat.

places Please

These mats are made from old placemats found in a yard sale. However, with a little preparation, the mats were transformed with some carefully chosen cutouts.

You will need

Placemats

Masking tape

Enamel or oil-based paint

Vegetable prints

Plain white paper

Watercolors

Small, sharp scissors

All-purpose glue

Sealer (fixative)

Spray varnish

Labels from packaging can be used for cutouts; or, photocopy a vegetable, and then color it.

1 If your mats have a border around the central picture, it may suit the overall design to keep it intact as a border for the new images. If this is the case, mask off the border using masking tape. Make sure you tape the edge of the border as straight as it is possible to do so.

2 Paint the enamel or oil-based color over the center of the mat, obscuring the printed scene. You may need several applications of paint to completely block out the image; these mats needed three coats. Allow each coat to dry completely before applying the next.

3 Photocopy the images to be used on white paper and use a little watercolor to tint the prints. Use the paint sparingly with a damp, not soaking wet, brush, to avoid wrinkles. Allow to dry, then seal with charcoal, watercolor, or pastel fixative.

4 Rub a little glue onto the surface of the mat around the position where the prints are to be placed. Wet your finger with a little water and work it into the glue to provide a smooth, slippery surface to enable the cutouts to be glided into position and to allow for repositioning. Seal cutouts with a little fixative.

5 Varnish the mats using spray-on polyurethane varnish – this is easy to apply and there are no brushes to clean! Apply at least five coats of varnish, allowing each coat to dry completely before applying the next. Leave the mats to dry for at least four days before using even though the surface may appear dry.

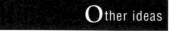

Other ideas

Use plywood for each placemat if you do not have any old ones. Back the reverse side with a piece of thin cork (such as a floor tile) or felt to protect the table surface.

fur*niT*ure

EditoR's ChAir

Newspapers offer a fascinating compendium of interesting typography. Capture some of your favorite printed phrases by decorating an office chair that will certainly make a statement.

You will need

A wooden or plastic chair

Newspapers

Scissors

Large sheet of white paper

Dry glue stick

Chinese white absorbent paper

Waterproof colored drawing inks

Jars or saucers for ink

Tweezers

Hairdryer (optional)

Craft glue

Clear matte varnish

Very fine steel wool

Varnishing wax

Polishing cloth

You can cut strips of newsprint in different ways. Tear it for a ragged, feathery effect or use pinking shears.

1 Choose a wooden or plastic chair that has flat surfaces to show off the newspaper. Collect a variety of newspapers, including foreign language ones (which can be purchased from rail stations and large news stands) to add interest.

2 Cut out interesting articles and headings to give a variety of typefaces and, using a dry glue stick, stick them onto a large sheet of white paper. Photocopy several times on Chinese absorbent paper. (This is available from art suppliers and you will have to cut it to size.) Carefully fold the photocopied Chinese paper into accordion (concertina) patterns and press them flat using a blunt knife to get sharply creased edges.

3 Take a selection of waterproof colored drawing inks and pour them into jars and saucers, one for each color. Carefully dip the corners of the folded Chinese paper into the colored inks, holding them with a pair of tweezers. Use two or three colors for each sheet. Allow the inks to become absorbed into the paper.

4 Carefully unfold the pleats and leave them to dry spread out on a sheet of newspaper – use a hairdryer to speed up this process.

5 When dry, cut the colored sheets into patterns and arrange them on the chair. Stick down with craft glue, smoothing out any air bubbles with your fingers and wiping off any excess. Allow to dry.

6 Apply clear matte varnish to the decorated chair and allow to dry overnight. When dry, lightly sand the chair with very fine steel wool. Dust with a clean, dry brush and revarnish.

7 When the second coat of varnish is dry, sand again and dust. Wax-varnish the chair and buff with a polishing cloth.

Other ideas

You could of course use newspaper to decorate any piece of wooden or plastic furniture that has plenty of flat surfaces. Instead of dyeing the paper you could leave the paper-covered chair to yellow in the sun before varnishing it.

Nursery Stool

This was a plain, untreated wooden stool which, while it was perfectly fine left in its natural state, looks even better with the addition of these delightful animal prints.

Wooden stool

Latex (emulsion) paint

Paintbrush

Animal prints

Small, sharp scissors

All-purpose glue

Sealer (fixative)

Acrylic-based varnish

1 Prepare the surface of the stool for painting. If it has been painted or varnished, remove these layers with an appropriate paint or varnish stripper, following the manufacturer's instructions and working outdoors if possible.

2 Cut out the images to be used with a pair of narrow-bladed scissors. Loosely arrange the pieces on the stool in a pleasing design prior to gluing them down.

3 Remove the cutouts, assembling them in the order they will be stuck on. Apply glue to the areas of the stool to be decoupaged. Work the glue into the surface with your finger. Dip your finger in water and work it into the glue to achieve a silky smooth surface.

4 Position the animal motifs over the glue and slide each one into place using your fingers and gentle pressure. The smooth surface of the glue enables the prints to be repositioned easily.

5 Remove excess glue from the surface using a small damp sponge. Work the sponge over the cutouts from the center of each print outward, rinsing the sponge in water when the glue builds up. Repeat until the surface is clear.

6 When the glue is totally dry, seal with fixative and leave to dry. Apply five or more coats of acrylic varnish, allowing each coat to dry before applying the next. Use the type of varnish made to protect the surface of cork or wooden floors for a tough, durable finish that is easily wiped clean. Build up as many layers of varnish as you have patience for, as a child's stool will be subjected to a great deal of wear and tear.

Furniture

You can have fun looking for different animal motifs to use in a child's room.

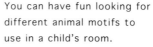

Select your images from a comic book or photocopy images from a favorite fairy story.

Coffee time

The strong bold text around the sides of this table uses text generated by a computer. If you do not have access to a computer you can enlarge bold text on a photocopy machine. A distressed paint finish is the ideal background for decoupage.

You will need

Small table

White household candle

Matte latex (emulsion) paint for base

Matte latex (emulsion) paint for top color

Medium-grade sandpaper

Text (computer or photocopy)

All-purpose glue

Small, sharp scissors

Sealer (fixative)

Acrylic varnish

1 Prepare the table for painting. If your table has existing layers of paint or varnish, remove with a commercial paint or varnish stripper. If it has been waxed, remove the wax with a pad of steel wool and turpentine. It is important to clean your table as thoroughly as possible as it will affect the final result.

2 Apply two coats of matte latex to the surface of the table, allowing each coat to dry completely. Rub a white household candle over the surface of the table top; this will resist the paint, making it easier to distress. Paint the second latex (emulsion) color over this and leave to dry.

3 Rub the surface of the table with medium-grade sandpaper. You will see that the top layer of paint comes away in areas with underlying wax, resulting in an attractive distressed paint effect. Cut strips of text from the sheets of copy.

4 Brush the glue onto the border of the table and lay the strips of text over it, smoothing from the center outward to avoid trapping any air bubbles. As the corners are laid over each other, cut the overlap into a neat miter. Apply a little more glue to re-stick if necessary.

5 Remove excess glue from the surface of the print and the table using a damp sponge. When the glue is thoroughly dry, use the fixative to seal the surface of the print. When this is dry, apply at least five coats of acrylic varnish to the surface of the table, allowing each coat to dry before applying the next.

Use old newspapers, even sheet music, to decorate small pieces of furniture.

Other ideas

Use English script around the table. If the table is to be used as a coffee table, you could print "everything stops for tea" or "all I want is a real cup of coffee" around the edge.

Sea AND *sheLLs*

This double-fronted cupboard was found in a local secondhand store, and although it needed a bit of hard work and elbow grease to remove old layers of varnish, it is transformed with this soft stippled paint finish and decoupage.

Wooden cupboard

Acrylic wood primer

Paintbrush

Latex (emulsion) paint

Acrylic paint in green and black

Acrylic latex (emulsion) glaze

Paint bucket (kettle)

Shell and fish pictures

Plain white paper

All-purpose glue

Sealer (fixative)

Acrylic varnish

Stippling brush

1 Prepare the cupboard for painting. Remove existing layers of paint or varnish using an appropriate stripper. Then rub first with coarse then medium-grade steel wool to remove any remaining traces. Remove old wax using a pad of steel wool soaked with turpentine. Fill any cracks or holes with an appropriate filler.

2 Apply a coat of acrylic-based wood primer to the cupboard. Then brush on two coats of your chosen base color latex (emulsion) paint. While this is drying, mix an acrylic glaze using a 1in (2.5cm) squeeze each of mid-green and black acrylic paint. Mix them together in the paint bucket with enough acrylic latex (emulsion) glaze to give the consistency of light (single) cream.

3 Allow the base color to dry completely. Photocopy the fish and shell pictures on white paper. Cut out the copies with a pair of sharp narrow-bladed scissors. Arrange the images over the cupboard into a satisfying design.

4 Apply a little glue over the area where the cutout is to be placed and work it to a silky smooth texture with your finger. Dip your finger into water and work it into the glue until you achieve the right consistency. Slide the cutouts in place and reposition them until you are satisfied with the overall effect.

5 Seal each cutout with a little fixative and allow to dry. Apply two coats of acrylic varnish allowing each coat to dry. Then brush the glaze completely over the cupboard using broad even strokes. Use a stippling brush (an old paste brush will do) to stipple the glaze. Work quickly and evenly as the glaze will dry quickly.

6 It looks effective if a little glaze is removed from the white areas of the photocopies; do this using a small piece of damp sponge. When you are satisfied with the stippled effect, leave the paint finish to dry. Protect with at least another three coats of acrylic varnish.

Other ideas

Use prints of small fishes around the edges of the cabinet and a larger shell in the center of the door panels.

Use a paintbrush to apply delicate color to this antique fish image.

COOk's CupboaRD

Look for images that are strongly linked to the kitchen, such as these knives and forks. Vegetable or fruit prints would also work well – seed catalogs and gardening publications are good sources of pictures.

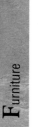

You will need

Wooden cupboard

Acrylic primer

Latex (emulsion) paint

Paintbrush

Tableware or vegetable prints

Plain white paper

All-purpose glue

Sponge

Sealer (fixative)

Acrylic varnish

Sandpaper

Dark brown furniture wax

Cotton cloth

Replacement handles/knobs

Oil-based paint for melamine top

1 Prepare the piece of furniture for painting. Remove existing layers of paint or varnish with the appropriate stripper. Follow the manufacturer's recommendations carefully, and work outdoors if possible. Paint the cupboard with acrylic primer and repair any cracks with filler.

2 When the filler has dried, apply at least two coats of your chosen latex (emulsion) base color. The final effect of applying the dark brown furniture wax will darken this color considerably, so bear this in mind when choosing the color.

3 Photocopy the decoupage images on white paper and seal the surface of each sheet using a charcoal, pastel or watercolor fixative. When the fixative is dry, cut out the images using a pair of scissors. Assemble the images on the cupboard door and arrange them into a design you are happy with.

4 Remove each cutout in turn and spread a little glue on the surface of the cupboard where the cutout is to be replaced. Dip your finger in water and rub it into the glue until you achieve a silky smooth surface. Position the cutout and slide it into position.

5 Wipe off the excess glue from around the cutout with a damp sponge, pressing from the center of each cutout to the edges. Allow to dry, then repeat this procedure until no glue remains on the surface. When dry, apply five coats of acrylic varnish to the cupboard. Allow each coat to dry before applying the next.

6 When the varnish is completely dry, scratch the surface with sandpaper. Apply colored wax to the surface of the furniture and rub vigorously. The wax will hold in the tiny scratches. Buff with a soft cotton cloth. Replace old handles with new ones and apply oil-based paint to cover the old melamine top.

Other ideas

Colour the photocopied images using colored crayons prior to sealing for an attractive tinted effect.

Fish, fruit, vegetables, tableware – there are a host of images that can transform your kitchen.

kitchen CUPboard

This cupboard began life as a basic kitchen utility cupboard; with a quick sanding and a new coat of paint, it was perfectly suited for decoupage.

Pretty flower prints add style to bedroom furniture.

1 Prepare the surface of the cupboard for painting. Old paint or varnish needs to be removed completely using a commercial paint stripper. Follow the manufacturer's instructions carefully and work outside if possible as the fumes can be unpleasant. If the furniture is waxed, rub it vigorously with mineral spirits and a pad of steel wool to remove the wax.

2 When the furniture is clean and dry, apply a coat of acrylic wood primer. Once dry, it will highlight any holes, dents, or cracks that need to be filled with an all-purpose filler. When the repair work is dry smooth the surface with sandpaper then apply your chosen base color latex (emulsion) paint. This color will darken slightly when the colored wax is applied.

3 Photocopy the lettering and botanical prints on white paper. Cut out the prints using a pair of sharp scissors with a small cutting edge. The botanical images should be cut with care and precision, particularly around delicate details such as the root system on the narcissus. If you are a beginner to decoupage, choose less complicated images to cut out. Cut the script into long, even strips.

4 Apply the glue to the surface of the cupboard (not to the paper) and spread it with your finger, working it into the surface. Dip your finger into water and work it into the glue to achieve a silky smooth surface on which you can slide the cutouts to arrange them.

5 Using a damp sponge lightly tamp the cutout, pressing and rolling the sponge from the center to the outside. Wipe away excess glue and use the same technique to apply the script around the sides of the cupboard door. Use a sharp craft blade to miter the edges. Remove glue from the surface using a sponge squeezed out in cool water. Seal the decoupage with fixative.

6 When totally dry, apply at least five coats of varnish, allowing each coat to dry thoroughly before applying the next. Then finely scratch the surface with steel wool and apply colored furniture wax, rubbing it in. Allow the wax to build up in some areas and add a little oil paint to the wax occasionally to create an interesting patina of age. Buff with a clean cotton cloth. Replace handles or knobs to finish.

Other ideas

As an alternative to using brown furniture wax, mix a little raw umber oil paint with a clear wax.

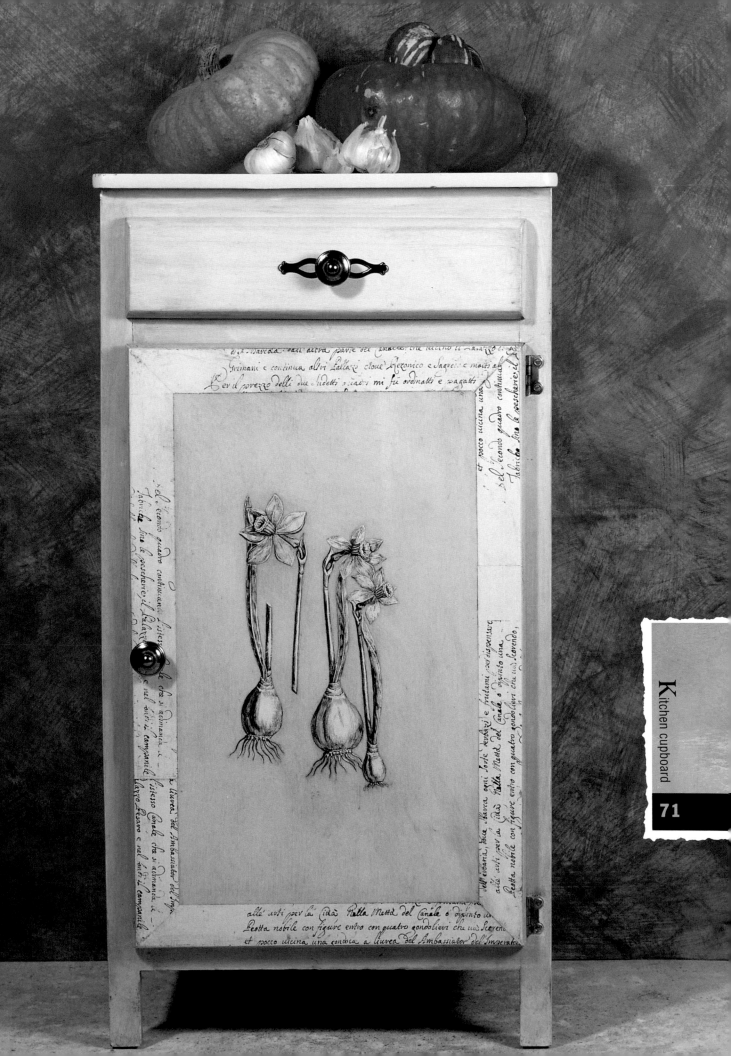

ChilD'S *Cup*BOARD

This child's cupboard was bought in a secondhand store, but you could adapt an existing storage unit in the same way.

You will need

Small cupboard

Sandpaper

Wood primer/sealer

Latex (emulsion) paint

Paintbrush

Wrapping paper

Small, sharp scissors

All-purpose glue

Small sponge

Acrylic varnish

Tassel

1 Prepare the piece of furniture for painting. If it is heavily painted or varnished strip it back to the base wood using paint/varnish stripper. Follow the manufacturer's instructions and work outside if possible. Smooth the surface using sandpaper.

2 Apply a coat of wood primer to the unit; this will highlight any cracks or holes that need to be filled. When dry, apply two coats of your chosen latex (emulsion) color. Cut out motifs from the wrapping paper using sharp scissors. Turn the paper, not the scissors, when cutting to ensure a smooth cut edge.

3 Apply a dab of glue in each area where a cutout is to be placed. Work the glue with your finger, rubbing it until it is silky smooth. Dip your finger in water and rub it into the glue to achieve this smoothness.

4 Position each cutout over the glued areas and slide into place; the worked glue allows for repositioning if required. Smooth each cutout down, pressing from the center outward to avoid trapping air bubbles. Allow the glue to dry.

5 Apply at least five coats of acrylic varnish, allowing each coat to dry thoroughly before applying the next. Use the type of varnish made to protect wood or cork floors. Replace the handle and add a tassel, if appropriate, for a finishing flourish.

These fishermen would be fun for a boy's room, or use simple, bright motifs for a nursery.

Other ideas

Use the same technique and motif to decoupage a headboard, storage chest, or any other piece of wooden furniture in the room to coordinate the whole effect.

Furniture

72

Shaker-Style Table

Traditional Shaker designs like these paired birds, hearts, and flowers, were used to decorate chests and cupboards. The designs were usually worked in paint, but the simple shapes make them ideal for cutting out of paper.

1 Prepare your wooden table or piece of furniture ready for painting. Use a paint stripper if necessary, then rub the table thoroughly using a pad of steel wool soaked with mineral spirits. Allow to dry, then apply a layer of white acrylic primer. When this is done, apply two coats of latex (emulsion) paint, preferably in one of the muted Shaker-inspired colors. Leave to dry.

2 Use a photocopier to enlarge or reduce the folk art designs to suit the size of the object you are decorating. The images used here were enlarged and copied on a color photocopier.

3 Carefully cut out the shapes with scissors, leaving small bridges to link the delicate areas together, if necessary, to prevent the cutouts from breaking when they are glued. Cut from the center of the design and work out toward the edges.

4 Dilute the glue with a little water until it has the consistency of thin cream, then brush it onto the table over the area to be covered by the cutout. Hold the cutout over the glued area, then lower the center section first, and tamp down the design from the center to the edges using a small, damp sponge.

5 Remove excess glue from the surface of the table using a gentle rocking movement with the sponge. Rinse the sponge in clean, cool water as the adhesive builds up, and continue to wipe off the excess glue until the surface is clear. Allow to dry thoroughly, at least overnight, but preferably for 24 hours.

6 Protect the surface of the decoupage with layers of varnish. You should use at least seven coats of varnish, but you can apply as many as 20 coats to give a really hard-wearing finish. Use water-based acrylic varnish or spray-on polyurethane varnish, allowing each coat to dry thoroughly before applying the next.

Other ideas

Use small parts of the design such as one bird, or a single flower or heart, to decorate a flowerpot or a picture frame to complement your table.

Shaker and other folk-art designs are very adaptable and can be used on both furniture and smaller items.

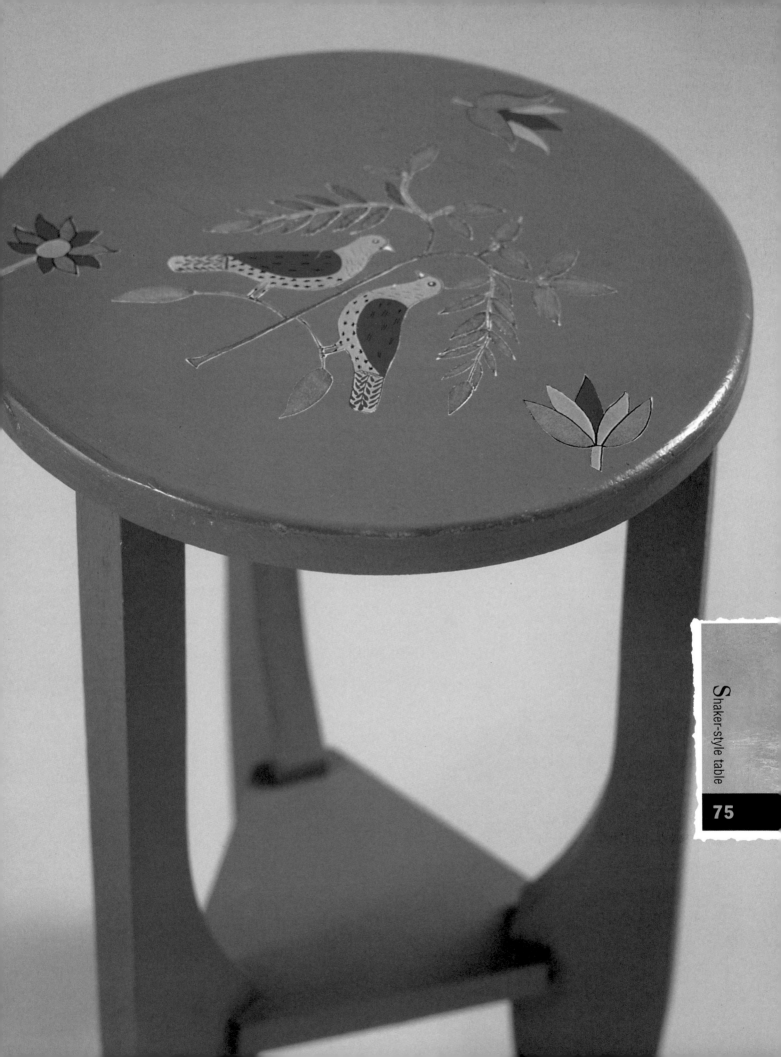

Ornaments, Boxes, & blanks

MAGAZINE rack

This traditionally shaped magazine rack has been decorated to dazzling effect with strips of a Japanese paper kite pasted over a bright pink construction paper (sugar paper) base. This will appeal to those who like a bold, colorful, adventurous style.

You will need

Wooden magazine rack

2 large sheets of bright pink construction (sugar) paper

A Japanese painted kite

Sheet of brightly colored Chinese printed paper

Wallpaper paste

Scissors

Water-based paint in yellow and blue

Small brush

Large brush

Very fine sandpaper

Acrylic satin varnish and brush

Choose your own style – you can be bold and modern or more traditional, depending on your taste.

1 Measure the long sides of the magazine rack and add ¾in (2cm) all around except for the top edge. Cut two pieces of pink construction (sugar) paper to this size. Apply wallpaper paste to the wooden surface and the back of the paper. Smooth the paper with your fingers to eliminate any air bubbles. This is important when working over a large surface. The paper will stretch a little when wet, but will shrink as it dries.

2 Lay the paper over the curved edge of the rack. Press the paper over the sharp edge of the wooden corners to make a fold. Remove paper, cut along these fold lines but leave ¾in (2cm) at the base edge to fold under and paste onto the base.

3 Paste the end papers carefully in place. Allow the pink paper to dry thoroughly.

4 Cut the Japanese kite into strips about 1½in (3.5cm) wide. You will need 16 strips all together. Mix them up so that when you paste them onto the magazine rack, the pattern is out of sequence.

5 Paste the strips evenly around the sides of the rack. Because of the shape of the end panels, the strips there will radiate out a little.

6 Cut a number of squares from the Chinese paper to fit at an angle between the strips already pasted down. Paste about six squares onto the pink background between each kite strip. Allow to dry.

7 Paint the inside of the rack with two coats of blue paint and the edge with two coats of yellow paint, allowing each coat to dry before applying the second. This makes a jazzy distinguishing line between the busy decoupage decoration and the vibrant blue interior.

8 Rub down the paint very lightly with fine sandpaper. Remove all dust and then varnish the whole rack with about six coats of acrylic satin varnish for protection. Allow each coat to dry before applying the next.

Other ideas

Magazine racks give plenty of scope for trying out different creative ideas. You could use pictures cut from magazines, newspaper cutouts, or photocopies of old bookplates and other reading themes.

Ornaments, boxes, & blanks

Grecian Vase

Create your own museum piece using a classic-shaped terracotta pot decorated with Greek illustrations.

You will need

- **Terracotta vase/urn**
- **Medium-grade sandpaper**
- **Clean, dry paintbrush**
- **Greek vase illustrations**
- **White paper**
- **Dry glue stick**
- **Scissors**
- **Terracotta-color drawing ink**
- **Craft glue**
- **Black India ink or vinyl silk latex (emulsion) paint**
- **Clear matte varnish and brush**
- **Very fine steel wool**
- **Varnishing wax**
- **Polishing cloth**

1 If the surface of your terracotta pot is rough, sand it smooth using medium-grade sandpaper. Dust with a clean, dry brush.

2 Photocopy the black-and-white Greek illustrations on white paper. Cut out selected images and position them economically on a large sheet of white paper and glue in place using a dry glue stick. Re-photocopy them.

3 Brush a wash of terracotta-color waterproof drawing ink over the images and allow to dry. This gives the images a more authentic "ancient" look. Cut out the tinted images accurately using small, sharp scissors. To give a smooth line, turn the paper, not the scissors, when cutting out.

4 If the vase/urn is glazed, apply a coat of vinyl silk paint; if it is unglazed terracotta, use black India ink. Allow to dry.

5 Apply craft glue to the selected images and stick to the painted vase/urn, wiping off any excess glue with a lightly dampened cloth. Allow to dry.

6 Apply clear matte varnish to the entire vase/urn and allow to dry overnight. Lightly sand using very fine steel wool and dust with a clean, dry brush. Revarnish and allow to dry. Sand again with the steel wool.

7 Dust with a clean, dry brush and apply oil color varnishing wax. Buff with a soft cloth.

Other ideas

If the pot or vase you wish to use is made of plastic, paint it with black vinyl silk paint instead of India ink. Visit museums to get more ideas about the colors and images to use.

Classical Greek patterns included acanthus leaves, squares, and spirals.

Classic PLAnter

Classic black-and-white architectural details give a touch of grandeur to an otherwise plain, ordinary terracotta pot which would probably remain outside in its natural state.

You will need

- **Terracotta plant pot**
- **Latex (emulsion) paint in green and white**
- **Paintbrush**
- **Plastic bags**
- **Pictures of architectural detailing**
- **Plain white paper**
- **Small, sharp scissors**
- **All-purpose glue**
- **Sponge**
- **Sealer (fixative)**
- **Acrylic varnish**
- **Clear furniture wax**
- **Artist's oil paint in white**
- **Fine steel wool**

1 Apply green latex (emulsion) paint to the plant pot. A solid base coat is needed, so it may require two coats. Paint inside the planter to a depth of approximately 4in (10cm).

2 When the base color is dry, apply the white paint to the planter. Dab a crumpled plastic bag (the thinner the better) first into the paint and then onto the surface of the pot. Build up the pattern gradually and keep turning the plastic to create an irregular pattern. Apply more green in the same way until you have a pleasing effect.

3 Allow the planter to dry completely. Photocopy the architectural detailing on white paper and cut out using small, sharp scissors. You need enough prints to cover the diameter of the planter. Apply glue to the back of the photocopies, not the pot, to avoid spoiling the painted surface.

4 Allow the glue to dry, then seal the copies with a fixative (charcoal, pastel, or watercolor fixative is available from art suppliers). When this is dry, apply at least five coats of acrylic varnish to protect and enhance the decoupage.

5 Color a little clear furniture wax with white oil paint and rub it into the surface of the planter using a small pad of fine steel wool. The wax gives a soft cloudy finish to the finished pot. Although natural terracotta is a porous material, do not plant anything directly in the pot once it is decorated, since the moisture will react against the applied decoration. Insert a plastic plant pot to avoid damage.

Other ideas

Paint the plant pot first with a suitable paintbrush. Use decorative architectural motifs.

Apply only the white paint, allowing the natural terracotta color to show through as the base color.

B○X Clever

This useful container can be used for all sorts of odds and ends. The same style of decoration would look good applied around the sides of a deep-sided butler's tray or a country-style basket.

You will need

Wooden box

Wood dye (if needed)

Pictures of architectural detailing

White paper

Small, sharp scissors

All-purpose glue

Sealer (fixative)

Acrylic varnish

Medium-gauge steel wool

Clear furniture wax

Oil paint in blue

Polishing cloth

1 If your chosen container is natural wood, you may wish to stain it with a colored wood dye. Make sure the container has been cleaned of any old paint, varnish, or old waxed layers. Apply the dye evenly to all the surfaces and allow to dry completely.

2 Enlarge or reduce your chosen architectural images on the photocopier. Print enough copies on white paper to go around your container. Cut out the architectural details from the photocopy paper using small, sharp scissors and arrange them around the container until you are satisfied with the overall design.

3 Spread the all-purpose glue over the area where the images will be placed and work the glue with your finger until it is silky smooth. Dip your finger in water and work it into the glue to achieve the right smoothness. Slide the prints in place; the silky finish allows the print to be repositioned.

4 Seal the surface of each print with a little fixative (available from art suppliers). When dry, apply at least five coats of acrylic varnish, allowing each to dry completely before applying the next.

5 When the final coat of varnish is dry, scour the surface with a pad of medium-gauge steel wool. Use a pad of fine-gauge steel wool to rub in a little clear furniture wax tinted with blue oil color (the two combine as they are rubbed in). Buff with a soft cotton cloth to finish.

Other ideas

Classical detailing creates an original box. You can use sandy yellow oil paint to tint the furniture wax.

Instead of blue oil paint, try other ocean colors such as aqua green and sandy yellow to mix in with the clear furniture wax.

Pots of color

Hide an ugly plastic flowerpot in a brightly decorated cache pot which will show off your plants to their best advantage.

Flat-side cache pot

Wrapping paper

Scissors

Craft glue

Craft knife

Latex (emulsion) paint

Varnishing wax

1 First find a suitably shaped cache pot, large enough to hold a standard-sized plant pot. A flat-sided pot is of course easier to decoupage. Then choose some wrapping paper designs. There is a wonderful choice of colors and textures available, and you may find one design which particularly inspires you. Floral themes are ideal for plant pots, but you can choose any design to suit your home.

2 Decide how you want the pattern to appear on the sides of the container. Using the pot as a template cut a piece of wrapping paper to cover a side, allowing an extra ⅛in (2–3mm) all around.

3 Apply a generous amount of glue to the paper and use a scrap of cardboard to spread it evenly, right up to the edges. Then glue the paper to the pot, rubbing it from the center outward with a clean cloth to make sure it is stuck down right up to the edges. When it is dry, carefully trim the extra paper with a craft knife and then go on to the next panel.

4 When all four sides have been covered, decide what color to paint the feet and inside; the edge could be painted in a contrasting color. This pot is black with a yellow painted edge.

5 When the pot is completely dry, apply two coats of varnishing wax to protect it. Place a tray inside to catch the water if your cache pot is made of wood. Leave the pot to dry in a well-ventilated, and dust-free room.

You can use brightly colored tissue paper instead of wrapping paper.Cut it with deckle-edged scissors.

Choose a different paper to go on each panel of the pot or cut shapes and flowers from gardening magazines and glue them over the wrapping paper. Add the fronts of seed packets to carry through the plant theme.

COMPACT STORAGE

Modern plastic packaging is efficient but often unsightly. You can hide away compact discs in boxes decorated with sheet music or pictures of your favorite musicians.

1 Choose a selection of sheet music and carefully cut them into pieces with small, sharp scissors. Arrange the paper pieces roughly on the blank box to make sure you have enough material, before sticking them down.

2 When you are happy with the arrangement, carefully glue them in place. Use a brush to spread the glue right to the edge of the pieces. Smooth the paper onto the box with your fingers to remove any air bubbles, then carefully wipe off any excess glue with a lightly dampened cloth. When the box is dry, check the corners and if necessary carefully re-stick them. Allow to dry.

3 Apply clear matte varnish to the outside of the box and allow to dry overnight in a dust-free place.

4 When dry, lightly sand the surface of the box using very fine steel wool, removing any lumps and bumps of varnish. Dust with a clean, dry brush. Revarnish and, when dry, sand smooth again.

Other ideas

The boxes could be themed with different pictures of pop stars or posters so that the contents of the boxes are instantly recognizable. To give the box an interesting crazed effect, you could use crackle glaze varnish after step 4.

Comics and old books with black-and-white illustrations are fun to use as source material – match the theme to the subject.

Ornaments, boxes, & blanks

CLock face

With cheap, modern quartz movements, you can have clocks all around your home, with clock faces to suit each different room.

You will need

Quartz clock movement

Masonite (hardboard)

Saw

Fine sandpaper

Illustrations or wrapping paper

Small scissors

Rubber stamp numbers (optional)

White paper

Craft glue

Crackle varnish

Oil paint in burnt sienna

Water-based matte varnish

Drill

Cutout photographs and prints of flowers look pretty.

1 Cut out your chosen shape for the clock face from the board using a saw. Smooth the edges of the wood using fine sandpaper. Place the clock face on a sheet of white paper and draw around it.

2 If you are using illustrations to decorate the clock face, photocopy them on white paper. This clock has an astrological theme taken from a book of astrological illustrations, and the stars are cut from sheets of wrapping paper.

3 Cut out the photocopied images and arrange all the materials inside the clock face paper outline. Decide if you want to have numbers on the clock. These numbers have been printed with a rubber stamp, but you could paint them on. Glue the shapes in place, then make a final photocopy on good quality white paper.

4 Apply glue to the back of the paper and spread it evenly with a scrap of cardboard. Place the photocopied clock face on the board clock face and smooth it gently with your fingers to remove any air bubbles. Paint the back and edges of the board.

5 If you want to apply crackle glaze to the clock face follow the manufacturer's instructions and paint on the first coat. Allow to dry, then apply a second coat. As the second coat dries, fine cracks will begin to appear. When thoroughly dry, rub a small amount of burnt umber oil paint into the cracks with a rag. Gently rub off the excess oil paint using a second rag and the flat of your hand to leave a residue in the cracks. Leave at least a day for the oil paint to dry. Coat the whole face and back with matte varnish.

6 Drill a hole in the center for the clock spindle and attach the hands and quartz movement.

Other ideas

Instead of putting numbers on the clock face, why not mark each hour with a picture of a butterfly or a flower, or choose a cake for a kitchen theme? Finish a floral clock with a huge flower in the center. Look through color magazines and at wrapping paper for inspiration.

hat BOX

Even if you don't wear hats, this boldly designed hat box will be useful as an unusual storage container. The clever contrast between paper lace trim and photocopied images of 19th-century hat and handbag designs is very striking.

You will need

Cardboard hat box, 14in (35cm) diameter and 8in (20cm) deep

Brown and black paper 6in (16cm) squares

Metal ruler

Craft knife

Cutting mat

Black-and-white illustrations

Sepia ink

Paintbrush

Small scissors

Wallpaper paste

3¼yd (3m) lacy paper ribbon

Matte acrylic varnish

Use lacy paper ribbon and pastels or bright, vibrant colors.

1 Using a metal ruler and craft knife on a cutting mat, cut the four brown and three black squares into quarters, i.e. 3in (8cm) squares. Draw two lines at right angles across the center of the box lid.

2 Mix a small amount of wallpaper paste. Starting with a brown square, paste it carefully onto the middle of the lid, lining it up with the pencil lines. Apply the paste both to the lid and to the back of the square. Smooth out any air bubbles.

3 Continue to glue the black and brown squares onto the lid in a checkerboard design. Lap the squares over the edges of the lid slightly. Cut strips of black paper to fit around the edge of the lid and glue in place.

4 Cut four squares of black and four squares of brown paper in half and paste in a striped design around the sides of the box. Paste a black strip around the top of the box base (this will be covered by the lid). Allow to dry.

5 Measure the paper ribbon and paste around the edge of the lid as shown. Paste half onto the side of the lid and half on top of the lid (snip it to fit). Cut another length of ribbon in half lengthwise and paste it around the base of the lid and around the base of the box. Allow to dry.

6 Select old illustrations from books and magazines and make enlarged photocopies. Tint the images by brushing on a wash of diluted sepia ink. Allow to dry and cut out carefully with the small scissors. To achieve a smooth outline, turn the paper, not the scissors, when cutting out.

7 Arrange the illustrations on the lid and side of the box, spacing them out to show the background. Paste carefully in place and smooth out any wrinkles or air bubbles with your fingers. Finally, apply at least four coats of varnish.

Other ideas

Hat boxes look good stacked up in a tower in descending sizes. Choose a different theme for each box, but keep to the same sepia coloring throughout to link the themes.

taPE That

Fed up with seeing ugly videotapes lying around the television set? Then buy plain boxes and decorate them with magazine pictures of your favorite films and programs.

1 Select pictures from magazines or wrapping paper and carefully cut them out with small, sharp scissors. It is easier to turn the paper, not the scissors, when cutting out detailed designs. Loosely arrange the pictures on the box to make sure you have enough material before gluing them. Use the larger pictures for the background, saving smaller pieces to fill in the gaps.

2 When you are happy with your arrangement, glue them in place. Carefully wipe off any excess glue with a lightly dampened cloth. Make sure that the images are pressed down.

3 When the pictures are dry (about one hour), check that no corners or edges are unstuck. If so, carefully re-stick them and allow to dry. You can label the boxes using letters cut from magazines.

4 Apply clear matte varnish to the outside of the box and allow to dry overnight in a dust-free place.

5 When dry, lightly sand the surface using very fine steel wool, removing any lumps and bumps of varnish. Dust with a clean, dry brush. Revarnish and, when dry, sand smooth again.

6 After final sanding, wax the outside of the box using oil color varnishing wax and buff with a soft cloth.

Choose unusual eye-catching motifs for a strong statement.

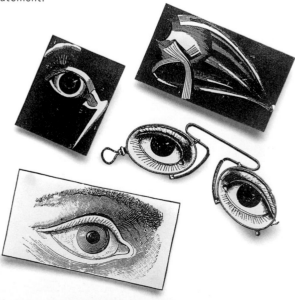

Other ideas

The boxes could be themed using different pictures for different videos so that you can easily recognize the contents. Children's comics could be used for covering a box for a child. Add old movie tickets to fill in small gaps between pictures.

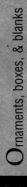

Ornaments, boxes, & blanks

Magic Lamp

The glass panels of this lamp are covered with opaque colored plastic to give a dramatic lighting effect.

Lamp with glass panels

Graph paper

Letratone film

Dishwashing liquid detergent

Compass

Ruler

Pencil

Stencil knife

1 Remove glass panels by bending up the metal flaps on the inside. Clean the glass with diluted liquid detergent. Leave to dry.

2 Work out your design on graph paper. This example uses a Mogul theme of arched windows. Place glass over your design and tape down.

3 Tape the first piece of Letratone in place on top of the glass. Using a pencil, ruler, and stencil knife, carefully cut out the Letratone in the appropriate shapes. Remove and cut out the other shapes in the appropriate colored Letratone. To make circles, use compasses (or draw around glasses or coins) to make accurate cardboard templates.

4 When all the Letratone shapes are cut out, peel off the backing and stick the shapes onto the glass panels. Carefully smooth down each piece to avoid air bubbles.

5 Turn the glass over and cover the back with Letratone (this masks the interior of the lamp and is optional). Rub down thoroughly to avoid air bubbles.

6 Replace panels in the lamp and bend retaining flaps back down.

Other ideas

You can also paint the base of the lamp to add to the new look. Letratone film comes in a choice of colors to suit a variety of design ideas. It is available from art suppliers.

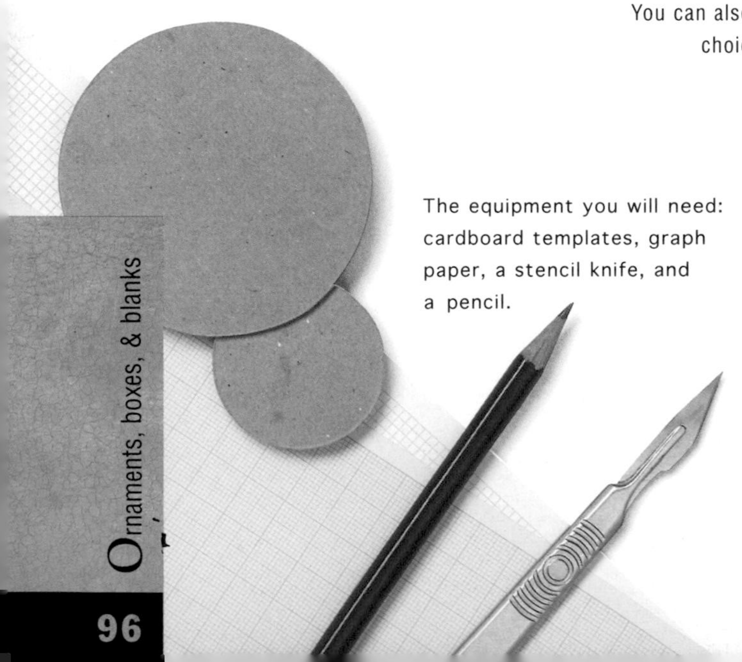

The equipment you will need: cardboard templates, graph paper, a stencil knife, and a pencil.

Ornaments, boxes, & blanks

Valentine Gift box

This pretty heart-shaped box would make a special Valentine gift filled with delicious handmade chocolates. The design on the lid is a papercut simply cut from textured gold paper.

1 Place the lid upside down on the back of the red poster paper and draw around it allowing about ⅛in (3mm) extra all around. Cut out.

2 For the side of the box, cut a strip of red paper long enough to wrap around and overlap at the join, and ⅝in (1.5cm) wider than its height.

3 Apply wallpaper paste to the lid and the back of the red paper. Position the paper on the lid and smooth down carefully, eliminating all air bubbles. Take care to stick the overlapping ⅛in (3mm) over the side of the lid. Allow to dry.

4 Cut a strip of gold paper to fit around the scalloped edge of the lid – cut it just big enough to wrap around the edge of the scallops. Paste in place and allow to dry.

5 Snip at ½in (12mm) intervals along the base edge of the red paper to be glued to the side of the box. Apply paste to the side of the box and to the back of the paper and smooth down carefully, overlapping slightly at the seam. Allow to dry.

6 Fold a 6¾in (17cm) square of gold paper in half, gold side inside and place a piece of carbon paper right side down on top. Trace or photocopy the template. Place the template with the straight edge against the fold of the gold paper.

7 Draw around the template design using a sharp pencil, pressing firmly to transfer the design.

8 Remove the template and carbon paper and very carefully cut around the pencil design using sharp scissors. Use a craft knife to cut any internal areas that are too difficult to reach with scissors. Always cut on a cutting mat for safety.

9 Carefully open the papercut and paste onto the lid of the box. Smooth it out with your fingers to remove any air bubbles, taking extra care as the papercut design is very delicate. Allow to dry.

10 Apply four or five coats of acrylic satin varnish, leaving each coat to dry thoroughly before applying the next.

You can use chocolate wrappers with the gold paper to link the decoration of the box with its contents.

aLL THAT glitTERs

This simple oval box has been cleverly transformed into a richly decorated jewellery box with a crazy patchwork design of sweet and chocolate wrappers. The simple copper tassel adds to the sumptuous effect.

You will need

Oval box

Selection of foil candy (sweet) wrappers

Craft glue

Glue brush

Satin acrylic varnish and brush

Gold paper

Copper tassel

1 Arrange the foil wrappers, balancing the colors, patterns, and shapes. Although a crazy patchwork effect looks random, it does need some planning.

2 When you are happy with your design, brush some glue onto a small area of the box lid. Glue the first piece of paper and carefully smooth it out. Cut the next piece of paper to shape if necessary and glue down, slightly overlapping the first piece.

3 Continue working in this way until the top of the lid is covered. Decorate the side of the lid with a little more formality. Stick alternate colored, patterned, and gold papers in even strips. For a neat edge, stick under the ends of the strips and finish off on the inside of the lid.

4 Line the inside of the lid with gold paper using craft glue to stick it in place. Repeat the crazy patchwork technique on the sides of the box, overlapping the top and base edges.

5 Cover the outside base of the box with gold paper and glue a strip all around the top of the inside of the box to make a neat seam with the glittery papers. Allow to dry.

6 Varnish the outside of the box with about six coats of satin acrylic varnish allowing each coat to dry before applying the next. Allow to dry.

7 Make a small hole in the center of the box lid. Push through the cord holding the copper tassel. Turn the cord around on itself on the inside of the lid to make a small spiral. Secure with craft glue.

Easter egg wrappers often have pretty patterns which give a rich, decorative effect; otherwise, use foil wrapping paper.

Other ideas

Easter egg wrappers are ideal for this project. If you can't wait to assemble enough wrappers, buy three or four sheets of foil wrapping paper and tear or cut it into smaller pieces

MOTHER HEN

This little hen has a lively folk art feel created by cutting and tearing a variety of colored and patterned papers to represent the feathers.

You will need

Two-tone paper: blue on one side, yellow on the other

Wallpaper paste

Pink origami paper

Chinese wrapping paper

Patterned wrapping paper in black and brown

Wooden chicken

Silk polyurethane varnish and brush

Fine sandpaper

1 Mix a small amount of wallpaper paste. Tear the blue and yellow two-tone paper into small pieces and paste onto the wooden chicken, yellow side up. This creates an interesting effect as the blue background is revealed along the tear line. Apply a small amount of paste to the chicken as well as to the paper. Smooth out any wrinkles with your fingers while the glue is still wet.

2 Tear two wing shapes from black wrapping paper and stick one on each side of the hen. Tear the brown wrapping paper into small pieces and paste them onto the wings.

3 Tear some pink origami paper into small pieces and glue them around the head area. Make the eye by cutting out a circle of yellow, ringing it with red and pasting a small black circle in the center. To create the feather effect, cut out "leaves and branches" from the brown paper and stick them around the head. Also use this paper to outline the yellow beak.

4 Tear more pink origami paper into small pieces and paste to the breast area. Add "feathers" of brown paper. Use Chinese paper to outline the breast area, to underline the wings and to surround the tail. Also paste pieces of Chinese paper along the top of the wings.

5 Decorate the hen's comb and neck with similar Chinese paper. Finally cut out larger "leaf" feathers and paste them onto the tail and around the neck.

6 When the paper and paste is thoroughly dry, apply four coats of silk polyurethane varnish, allowing each coat to dry before applying the next. Lightly sand the third coat to create a smooth finish.

A variety of colored and patterned papers can be used to create a lively, eye-catching design.

Other ideas

This is a freehand design, and the end result depends on your choice of colors and papers. Tearing the papers adds to the freehand look, but you could cut the papers if you prefer a neater effect.

ribbon box

The fluorescent pink wired ribbon is attached in a clever way so you don't need to untie it to open the present. The brightly decorated box can be kept for storing precious items.

You will need

Cardboard box with lid, 6¼in (16cm) square by 4in (10cm) deep

1 sheet of royal blue poster paper

Wallpaper paste

Half a sheet each of fluorescent paper in orange, yellow, and green

3¼yd (3m) fluorescent pink wired ribbon, 1⅜in (3.5cm) wide

Double-sided tape

Matte polyurethane varnish

Varnish brush

Scissors

Complete your ribboned bow with a sumptuous tassel.

1 Measure and cut royal blue paper to fit lid and sides of box.

2 Mix a small amount of wallpaper paste. Paste the paper onto the box, applying the paste both to the box and the back of the paper. Smooth it gently. Turn the edges over into the box and the inside of the lid.

3 Cut eight 2in (5cm) squares of green paper and paste two onto each side of the box, leaving a little more than a ribbon width in between.

4 Cut eight 1¼in (3cm) squares of orange paper and eight ¾in (2cm) squares of yellow paper. Paste the orange squares onto the green squares at an angle so that the corners intersect the long side. Do the same with the yellow squares.

5 For the lid cut four 2in (5cm) squares of orange, four 1¼in (3cm) squares of yellow and four ¾in (2cm) squares of green. Create the same pattern on the top of the lid as for the sides, gluing the squares down in a different color order, again leaving a ribbon width in between.

6 Cut strips of yellow paper ⅝in (1.5cm) by 2in (5cm) and paste them onto the side of the lid as shown. Paste small squares of orange paper at an angle on top of them.

7 Cut pieces of orange paper to line the inside of the box and the lid. Paste them on one at a time and stick in place. Allow the paper to dry.

8 Varnish the outside of the box with three coats of matte polyurethane varnish, allowing each coat to dry thoroughly.

9 Cut two lengths of ribbon long enough to go around the box and to tuck under the rim by about ¾in (2cm). Cut lengths of double-sided tape and stick them to the box where the ribbon is to be attached.

10 Loosely stick the ribbon onto the tape and tuck it under the rim. Cover the ends by pasting orange paper over the ends of the ribbon.

11 Apply the ribbon to the box lid in the same way, the two lengths long enough to tie a generous bow.

Other ideas

The advantage of using wired ribbon is that when you arrange the bow and ribbon ends, it stays in position. As an alternative, crèpe paper can be tied into a stiff bow.

Beam me Up!

This unusual briefcase is a cheerful and useful carry-all for those notes, letters and memoranda we have to take around with us. Children will also love it as a container for their school projects.

1 Select a suitable briefcase; a cardboard one is ideal. Spray the briefcase evenly with silver paint. Allow to dry thoroughly.

2 Select, and then photocopy, a variety of pictures illustrating the space age taken from magazines, comics and books.

3 Colour the photocopies with pencils, and then cut out the imagery carefully.

4 Position the cutouts to make an eye-catching design. The landscape effect at the base of the briefcase was created by overlaying the cutouts. Stick the cutouts onto the briefcase with the adhesive, taking care to remove any glue.

5 Seal cutouts with a little fixative. Varnish, to make it waterproof, using spray-on polyurethane varnish. Apply at least five layers of varnish and allow each layer to dry completely before applying the next. Leave the briefcase for at least four days before using even though the surface may seem quite dry.

Other ideas

Make this a jolly present for a friend or relative, with cutouts chosen to complement their interests. For example, flowers or vegetables would be suitable for a keen gardener or pictures of locomotives for a trainspotter.

For a different style, choose old fashioned motifs.

Ornaments, boxes, & blanks

106

fRuit SALad

This Matisse-inspired fruit bowl with its leaf cutouts in exotic summery colors will jazz up your kitchen table throughout the year. Pile it up with oranges, mangoes, bananas, and red apples.

Large ready-made papier-mâché fruit bowl, plain or painted

Selection of yellow and orange papers

Wallpaper paste

Craft knife

Origami paper in purple, orange, light and dark green, red, blue, and plum

Purple construction (sugar) paper

Small scissors

Gloss polyurethane varnish and brush

Pencil

Fine sandpaper

1 Mix a small amount of wallpaper paste. Tear the yellow and and shapes and carefully paste them all over the bowl, right up to the rim. Apply the paste both to the surface of the bowl and to the back of the paper. Stick down and smooth out any wrinkles or air bubbles with your fingers while the paste is still wet. Trim the papers along the edge of the bowl using a craft knife.

2 Draw leaf shapes on the back of the origami paper in rough oak and ash leaf style. If you do not have the confidence to draw the shapes freehand, find some real leaves to use as templates. Carefully tear around the pencil line – this creates a softer edge than cutting with scissors. Paste the leaf shapes onto the background, balancing the colors as you proceed.

3 Tear some colored "spots" from the same paper and glue onto the bowl between the leaves. Cover the sides and base of the bowl with purple construction (sugar) paper.

4 Use the small scissors to cut out pieces of plum-colored origami paper to fit around the rim of the bowl. Paste in position. When all the paper is thoroughly dry, apply three coats of gloss varnish. Sand the bowl with fine sandpaper and dust with a clean, dry brush. Apply a final coat of varnish and leave to dry in a well-ventilated room.

Instead of leaf shapes, choose fruit or vegetable shapes, or make the design completely abstract.

Ornaments, boxes, & blanks

Tear paper for irregular, freehand shapes or for a more precise line, such as the strawberry stalks, cut out with scissors.

CHILI hot

Almost anything made from papier-mâché would look good decorated with a pattern of decoupage cutouts. These quirky chili motifs are cut from a sheet of wrapping paper. Wrapping papers are often excellent sources of images.

You will need

Papier-mâché item

Wet-and-dry sandpaper

Latex (emulsion) paints

Paintbrushes

Wrapping paper

Small, sharp scissors

All-purpose glue

Sponge

Sealer (fixative)

Acrylic varnish

Fruit and vegetables make excellent subjects for decoupage. Use sandpaper to prepare the surface so that the cutouts adhere easily.

1 Prepare the papier-mâché object for decoupage. For an untreated item, apply a coat of paint. For an item that has been varnished rub the surface using damp wet-and-dry sandpaper to "key" the surface so the cutouts will stick.

2 Cut the images carefully from the wrapping paper following the outlines precisely to avoid jagged edges. Apply glue around the inside rim of the bowl and work it into the surface with your finger. Dip the end of your finger in water and work it into the glued surface to achieve a silky smooth surface.

3 Place each cutout in turn onto the glued surface and slide the motif into position; the slippery surface allows for repositioning. To achieve an even symmetry of chili peppers, apply each motif as if on a clock face, placing the 12, 6, 3, and 9 o'clock positions first, then filling in between the gaps.

4 Remove excess glue using a small dampened sponge, then tamp the motif, lightly pressing the sponge from the center outward. Rinse the sponge as the glue builds up and continue until the surface is clear. Allow to dry completely.

5 Apply a coat of protective sealer, such as charcoal, pastel, or watercolor fixative, available from art suppliers. Apply at least five separate coats of acrylic varnish, allowing each coat to dry thoroughly before applying the next. The more layers you build up, the better the overall effect will be.

Other ideas

Select a black-and-white image and hand-tint the fruit or vegetables using colored pencils. Seal with fixative before varnishing.

Index